STARS FROM THE EAST

(Irathiro)

ANTHONY MWANGI

Crony Trading LTD

Copyright © 2025 Anthony Mwangi — the BRANCH seated in Zion

All rights reserved.

No part of this publication may be reproduced, distributed, or transmitted in any form or by any means—electronic, mechanical, photocopying, recording, or otherwise—without the prior written permission of the author, except in brief quotations used in reviews or critical articles.

Scripture quotations are taken from the King James Version (KJV) of the Holy Bible, which is public domain.

This book is a prophetic work written and sealed in fire, dedicated to the restoration of divine truth and the awakening of Zion in the nations.

Cover Design & Visual Identity: White, Gold, Purple, Violet, and Blue — representing Purity, Glory, Royalty, Intercession, and Heaven.

ISBN: 978-1-918186-05-5

First Edition — 2025

I dedicate this book to the Bright and Morning Star, Jesus Christ, the Light who rose from the East and shall never set. To Him belongs all glory, for He is the true Irathiro — the Beginning and the End.

To the Holy Spirit, the Seal of the Sabbath and the Breath of the East Wind, who whispered these revelations line upon line and gave the light to see hidden things.

To Zion, the eternal mountain of God, the throne of stars, where the righteous shall shine forever.

To my beloved nation Kenya — the land of Irathiro, the rising place of the sun, whose destiny is to birth holy stars for the glory of Christ. May her sons and daughters shine as lights in a crooked generation.

And finally, to the Remnant Bride, scattered across the earth, who hear the call of the East Gate: "Arise, shine; for thy light is come, and the glory of the LORD is risen upon thee." (Isaiah 60:1).

May every page ignite the star within you, until you are found seated in Zion, clothed with the light of the Lamb.

"For the LORD shall arise upon thee, and His glory shall be seen upon thee."
— Isaiah 60:2 (KJV)

Eastward the light breaks.
The stars awaken from ancient silence.
Africa turns her face toward the dawn,
and Irathiro — the rising — begins.

From Eden to Zion, from Mount Kenya to the heavens,
the same voice speaks: "Let there be light."
And the light becomes nations,
the nations become stars,
and the stars return home to God.

HANNAH MWANGI

CONTENTS

Title Page
Copyright
Dedication
Epigraph
Preface
Introduction
Prologue
Foreword
PART I   1
Chapter 1   3
Chapter 2   8
Chapter 3   13
PART II   17
Chapter 4   18
Chapter 5   22
Chapter 6   26
PART III   31
Chapter 7   32
Chapter 8   36
Chapter 9   41
Chapter 10   45

Chapter 11	49
Chapter 12	53
PART V	57
Chapter 13	58
Chapter 14	62
PART VI	67
Chapter 15	68
Chapter 16	72
Chapter 17	74
Chapter 18	76
PART VII	79
Chapter 19	80
Chapter 20	83
Chapter 21	86
PART VIII	89
Chapter 22	90
Chapter 23	95
Chapter 24	98
BONUS PART	101
Chapter 25	102
Chapter 26	105
Chapter 27	108
Chapter 28	111
Chapter 29	114
Chapter 30	117
Chapter 31	120
Chapter 32	123
Prayer	126

Books By This Author	129
About The Author	135
PROPHETIC EPILOGUE: THE SCROLL OF IRATHIRO	137
Afterword	141
Acknowledgement	143
The Rising of Irathiro	145

PREFACE

Prophetic Preface — The Rising of Irathiro

In the beginning, God planted His garden eastward in Eden — a whisper of origin, a direction of light. From that first sunrise, every covenant, every promise, every star was drawn eastward, toward awakening. Irathiro — "the rising" — is not a place alone; it is a prophecy, a heartbeat that began in Eden and now echoes in Africa.

The story of the stars is the story of man's return to light. From Abraham's gaze upon the heavens, counting stars as heirs, to the vision of John beholding a Woman crowned with twelve, the testimony remains: God writes His promise in the firmament. Each constellation speaks of covenant; each dawn reminds the world that glory still rises in the East.

This book is born from that dawn. It gathers the hidden seed of Genesis, the fire of Pentecost, and the shining of Zion into one unbroken revelation — that the Spirit has chosen a people, a mountain, a moment. Kenya, the mountain nation of whiteness, stands as a final witness of Irathiro: the east star of the earth, where prayer becomes light and the nations behold the glory of the Lamb.

The rising is not new; it is ancient light remembered. It is the Sabbath of nations, the rest of the Spirit returning to its throne. And as the Bright Morning Star ascends, His reflection multiplies — sons and daughters shining as constellations of fire.

Irathiro has risen. The East has spoken. The stars are home again.

INTRODUCTION

The Revelation of Irathiro

Every generation is marked by a sound. In ours, it is the sound of the East awakening. Prophecies once sealed in parchment are now speaking through nations, mountains, and rivers. The Spirit is gathering the scattered lights of Israel, forming again the constellation of Zion — and Africa stands at the center of this divine rising.

Irathiro means "east" in the Kikuyu tongue, but its essence reaches beyond direction — it means *the place of God's appearing, the dawning of His glory.* From Eden's eastward garden to Ezekiel's East Gate, from the Mount of Olives to Mount Kenya's snowy crown, the Word has kept one rhythm: *the glory of God rises in the East.*

This revelation is not new light; it is ancient light restored. Kenya's very name, drawn from a mountain whose whiteness mirrors divine purity, declares its prophetic role: the mountain-nation set apart for prayer, revival, and the final outpouring of the Spirit. The rivers flowing from its slopes — Tana, Ewaso Nyiro, and others — mirror the heavenly streams that make glad the city of God (Psalm 46:4). Thus, the physical landscape itself becomes a living parable of Zion's throne.

The Scroll of Irathiro unfolds this mystery — that God has hidden in Africa the echo of Israel's destiny, the sign of His covenant to gather His people once more in light. It reveals how the Sabbath

Spirit, the Bride, and the constellation of holy stars converge in one eternal decree: that the Bright Morning Star shall reign from Zion, and His glory shall cover the earth as the waters cover the sea.

This is not history retold but prophecy fulfilled — the unveiling of the final eastward movement of God. The book you hold is a map, a mirror, and a mandate. It invites every reader to rise as a star in the Lamb's constellation, to take their place in the divine government of light.

For the East has risen. The throne has spoken.
And the stars are gathering once more for the marriage of heaven and earth.

PROLOGUE

The Dawn of Irathiro

Before there was a nation, there was a light.
Before there was a temple, there was a mountain — eastward, white with promise.

In that light, the Word spoke: *"Let there be morning."*

From Eden's gate to Mount Moriah, from Sinai's fire to the Mount of Transfiguration, every ascent has pointed toward one revelation — that God meets man in the rising.

The East is not mere geography; it is the posture of divine awakening, the place where darkness yields to the voice of light.

Across ages and continents, this eastward current has carried the covenant flame. It moved from Adam's garden to Abraham's altar, from Zion's hill to the upper room of Pentecost — until it reached the silent slopes of Africa, where another mountain stood waiting. *Mount Kenya — Kirinyaga — the Mountain of Whiteness.* There, creation itself bears witness to the pattern of God: eastward rivers flowing, snow upon its head, and light resting on its crown.

In that image, the mystery of *Irathiro* was sealed — the prophecy that in the end of days, the rising of God's glory would begin once more from the East, from a mountain that bears His likeness. Kenya would become more than a nation; it would become a sign — a typology of Israel reborn in Spirit.

This is the story of that rising. Not of politics or borders, but of stars — holy ones awakened, wandering ones judged, constellations aligned beneath the throne. It is the story of the Bride clothed with the sun, crowned with twelve stars, standing in travail as the kingdoms of this world yield to the Kingdom of the Lamb.

When you read these pages, do not read them as history alone. Read them as witness — as the unveiling of a scroll written long before time began, now opened in fire. For *The Scroll of Irathiro* is not just written with ink, but with light — the light of the East that never sets.

The dawn has come.
The stars are stirring.
The Lamb reigns from Zion, and His fire is rising from Irathiro.

FOREWORD

The Fire That Rises from the East

There are moments in history when heaven bends close, when the veil between time and eternity thins, and a sound moves through creation like the first wind before dawn. *The Scroll of Irathiro* belongs to such a moment.

This book does not come as theory or theology—it comes as testimony. It declares that the same God who once walked in Eden, thundered from Sinai, and spoke from Zion, has not forgotten the continent that bears His hidden seal. Africa, the sleeping womb of prophecy, now awakens. And at her heart stands Kenya—*Irathiro*, the East—rising as a witness that the glory of God will again cover the earth as the waters cover the sea.

In these pages, Anthony Mwangi — *the Branch seated in Zion* — weaves a revelation that restores the world's forgotten compass. He shows that the East is not merely where the sun rises, but where the Spirit speaks first. He traces how the rivers from Mount Kenya mirror the streams from the throne of God, how the stars of Abraham's promise now shine over Africa's sky, and how the Sabbath fire that once burned in Zion now rests upon a mountain called Whiteness.

This work is not meant to entertain. It is meant to awaken. It summons prophets, priests, and kings from every nation to remember their starry origin and take their place in the constellation of the Lamb. For the kingdoms of this world have long borrowed light from Babylon's lamps, but the true light, the holy fire, the Irathiro glory, has returned to the East.

May every reader hear the call that echoes between these lines: *Rise, for your light has come, and the glory of the Lord is risen upon you.*

The fire is already rising.
The scroll is open.
And from the mountain of the East, the stars of Zion begin to sing.

PART I

THE RISING EAST — ORIGINS OF LIGHT AND WAR

CHAPTER 1

The Mystery of Irathiro

1. The Word in Kikuyu Tongue

The Kikuyu word Irathiro means the East, the rising place of the sun. But beyond geography, it is prophecy. It carries the mystery of first light — the dawn where darkness breaks, where beginnings are birthed, and where destinies are tested.

For the East is not neutral. It is both **glory and warfare**. The same East that opens Eden's gates is the East that stirs rebellion. The same East that ushers God's glory is the East that gives rise to counterfeit stars. To understand *Irathiro* is to understand the tension of light and darkness, the war of stars from the beginning until the end.

2. Genesis — Eden Eastward

"And the LORD God planted a garden eastward in Eden; and there he put the man whom he had formed" (**Genesis 2:8**).

The first location God names in Scripture is the **East**. Eden was not random — it was placed *eastward* as a sign that God's throne of glory faces East. Eden's East was the first courtroom, the first altar, the first gate where man walked with God in the cool of the day.

But when man sinned, that same East became a place of **judgment and exile**. Cherubim with a flaming sword were set *at the east of Eden* to guard the way to the Tree of Life (**Genesis 3:24**). What does this mean? That the East is both the **gate of access** and the **gate of denial**. Whoever masters the East masters the entry to God's glory.

3. Cain — Wandering Stars from the East

When Cain murdered Abel, the Bible says: *"Cain went out from the presence of the LORD, and dwelt in the land of Nod, on the east of Eden"* (**Genesis 4:16**).

The first murderer became the first **wandering star** (**Jude 1:13**). Driven East, he built a city in rebellion, a counterfeit constellation. From Cain's East lineage came Lamech, who perfected violence and corruption. The East thus became associated not only with beginnings but also with the rise of **counterfeit stars** — men and systems carrying false light.

4. Babel — The Eastward Rebellion

"And it came to pass, as they journeyed from the east, that they found a plain in the land of Shinar; and they dwelt there" (**Genesis 11:2**).

The builders of Babel carried the spirit of Cain. They gathered eastward to build a tower that would reach the heavens — a false star-gate, a counterfeit Irathiro. Babel was the womb of astrology, of false constellations, of stars that rebel against the true Light.

Here the mystery deepens: every counterfeit rising is an attempt to **control the East Gate**. Every false altar seeks to block the true stars from shining.

5. Abraham — The Promise of Stars

God called Abraham out of the East (Ur of the Chaldees) to birth a new constellation. *"Look now toward heaven, and tell the stars, if thou be able to number them… so shall thy seed be"* (**Genesis 15:5**).

Here God reveals the warfare of stars: Abraham's lineage would not just be people, but **holy stars**, shining in covenant. Yet even Abraham's story is entangled with East warfare: Ishmael (a son of the East, *Genesis 16*) became a line of contention, producing stars of strife that battle Israel to this day.

6. The Double Nature of Irathiro

From these beginnings we see a pattern:

- Eden East — Glory Gate.
- Cherubim East — Judgment Gate.
- Cain East — Wandering Stars.
- Babel East — Counterfeit Rising.
- Abraham East — Covenant Stars.

Thus, *Irathiro* is both **a promise and a battleground**. The true

Irathiro births holy stars destined for Zion. The false Irathiro births wandering and rebellious stars destined for judgment.

7. Prophetic Warfare of the Stars

Beloved, the mystery of Irathiro is this: every generation produces rising stars. Some rise in holiness to testify of Christ, the Bright and Morning Star. Others rise in rebellion, shining for a season before being cast into outer darkness.

Isaiah saw both sides: *"Arise, shine; for thy light is come"* (**Isaiah 60:1**) — yet also, *"How art thou fallen from heaven, O Lucifer, son of the morning!"* (**Isaiah 14:12**).

The East is therefore a **battlefield of light**. Whoever controls the East controls the destiny of nations. This is why kingdoms rise in the East, why wise men came from the East, and why even in the last days, the rising of the sun marks the seal of the servants of God (**Revelation 7:2**).

8. Irathiro — Africa's Prophetic Code

In Kikuyu prophecy, *Irathiro* is not merely geography — it is destiny. Kenya, the land of the rising sun, carries a prophetic marker that cannot be ignored. Just as God placed Eden eastward, so has He placed within Africa a seed of rising stars.

The question is not whether stars will rise from Irathiro — they already are. The question is: **will they be holy or counterfeit?** Will they shine in righteousness, or wander in rebellion?

9. Sealing the Revelation

The mystery of Irathiro reveals three eternal truths:

1. The East is the **gate of beginnings**.

2. The East is the **battlefield of stars**.

3. The East is the **throne gate of God's glory**.

This first chapter sets the tone: throughout Scripture and history, the East marks the rise of stars — some holy, some false. And in these last days, God is calling His remnant to arise as the **true stars of Irathiro**, shining in the midst of darkness, sealed for Zion's glory.

Activation Decree:

"I arise as a holy star from Irathiro. I renounce the wandering path of Cain, the rebellion of Babel, and the counterfeit altars of false light. By the blood of Jesus, the Bright and Morning Star, I am sealed in Zion's constellation. I shine forever in the East Gate of God's glory."

CHAPTER 2

Eden Eastward — The Courtroom of First Light

1. The Planting of Eden Eastward

"And the LORD God planted a garden eastward in Eden; and there he put the man whom he had formed" (Genesis 2:8).

The first deliberate action of God concerning man's dwelling was **to plant Eden eastward**. This was no random direction. The East represents:

- **First Light** — the dawning of God's Word, the beginning of revelation.
- **First Throne** — Eden was the initial seat of divine government on earth.
- **First Courtroom** — the East Gate became the place of access, judgment, and covenantal encounter.

Eden eastward was not merely a garden — it was a **living temple**, where man functioned as priest, witness, and star. The East was the courtroom entrance, where light testified against darkness.

2. Adam as the First Star-Clothed Man

Adam was created as the **first star-clothed witness** in God's courtroom. Before sin, his garment was not animal skin, but **light**.

- **Spiritology**: His spirit radiated the glory of the Creator — he bore the reflection of the Bright and Morning Star. He was clothed in uncreated light, functioning as a star in the East Gate of Eden.
- **Soulogy**: His soul carried alignment — mind, will, and emotions perfectly synchronized with God's law. He was a living decree, shining as a star-witness of God's authority.
- **Physiology**: His body was a temple, energized by the Tree of Life. He was the first constellation — spirit, soul, and body aligned in divine order, a microcosm of the East Gate.
- **Theology**: Theologically, Adam stood in the East as a prophetic foreshadowing of Christ — the Second Adam, who would later be transfigured as light, and rise as the eternal Morning Star.

Adam's placement in the East revealed man's original mandate: to **judge, govern, and shine** as a star-witness in God's earthly courtroom.

3. Cain Driven Eastward — The Birth of Wandering Stars

When Cain murdered Abel, the blood cried out from the ground. Court convened. God summoned Cain into judgment at the East Gate of Eden.

The verdict was exile. *"And Cain went out from the presence of the*

LORD, and dwelt in the land of Nod, on the east of Eden" (**Genesis 4:16**).

Cain became the prototype of **wandering stars** (*Jude 1:13*):

- **Spiritology**: His spirit was cut off from divine alignment. Instead of light, darkness clothed him. His "star" burned dim and began to wander.
- **Soulogy**: His soul was filled with restlessness. He could not find Sabbath rest — his emotions and mind turned chaotic.
- **Physiology**: His body bore a mark, a physical sign of judgment, sealing him as a false star destined for exile.
- **Theology**: He became the founder of counterfeit altars and cities — a shadow of Babel, the kingdom of rebellion.

Thus the East, once a gate of glory, became in Cain's lineage a gate of rebellion. His exile eastward was prophetic: whenever man rejects God's Word, he is driven into a counterfeit Irathiro — a rising of false light that leads to destruction.

4. The East Gate as Courtroom

Why does God position the **Cherubim with flaming sword at the East of Eden** (Genesis 3:24)? Because the East is not just a direction — it is the **Courtroom of First Light**.

- Every **access** to God passes through the East Gate.
- Every **judgment** against rebellion is executed at the East Gate.
- Every **witness** of light vs. darkness is tested at the East Gate.

The East Gate is where heaven's decrees enter earth. This is why Ezekiel later sees the glory of the LORD coming *from the East* (**Ezekiel 43:2**). It is the throne gate of divine verdicts.

5. The Pattern of Star Warfare in Eden

From the beginning, the East reveals two orders of stars:

1. **Adam — the Star-Clothed Man** (holy star, aligned with God's glory).
2. **Cain — the Wandering Star** (rebellious star, cast out from God's presence).

This duality repeats throughout Scripture:

- Eden Eastward: Adam shines, Cain falls.
- Babel Eastward: Nimrod rises, God scatters.
- Israel Eastward: the tabernacle faces East, God's glory enters.
- Christ Eastward: the Star rises in Bethlehem, Herod's false star falls.
- Last Days Eastward: righteous stars shine, fallen stars are cast down.

6. Prophetic Application — Standing in the East Gate

Beloved, every believer must choose where to stand in the East Gate:

- As **Adam restored in Christ**, clothed in light, a true star-witness in God's courtroom.
- Or as **Cain**, wandering, restless, marked by rebellion, cast into exile.

The East Gate is still open. The flaming sword of judgment is also the flaming star of grace. Christ, the Bright and Morning Star, has opened the way back into the East of Eden — Zion, the eternal dwelling of God.

Sealing Revelation of Chapter 2

- **Spiritology**: Eden Eastward is the spiritual gate of light and judgment.
- **Soulogy**: Man's soul was designed to align with the rhythm of East glory (Sabbath rest).
- **Physiology**: Man's body was clothed in light as a star-temple of God.
- **Theology**: The East Gate is the courtroom of God's government on earth, fulfilled in Christ the Bright Star.

Activation Decree:
"I stand in the East Gate of Eden, redeemed by the blood of the Lamb. I refuse the exile of Cain and the restlessness of wandering stars. I embrace the light-clothing of Christ, the Bright and Morning Star. I declare that my spirit, soul, and body are aligned in Zion's courtroom. I am a holy star of Irathiro, sealed for God's glory."

CHAPTER 3

Babel and the Counterfeit Rising

"And they said, Go to, let us build us a city and a tower, whose top may reach unto heaven, and let us make us a name…" — Genesis 11:4

1. The Stars of Nimrod and Shinar

- **Spiritology**: Nimrod, whose name means *"we shall rebel"*, was not just a hunter of beasts but of souls. He hunted men to bind them under his dominion. His kingdom began in Shinar — a plain in the East. In prophetic language, Shinar is the valley where stars that fell attempted to rise again by their own strength.

- **Soulogy**: Man, created as a witness in the heavenly courtroom, now sought to establish his own identity apart from God. The desire for a "name" (shem) was not just for fame, but for spiritual permanence — they wanted to engrave themselves in heaven without submission to the true Light.

- **Physiology**: The tower was not merely architecture; it

was an attempt to build a *cosmic ziggurat* that linked the human body to counterfeit constellations. Every brick was a rebellion, every stone an idol, every height a mockery of Mount Zion.

- **Theology**: Babel was not just a city — it was a counterfeit Jerusalem. Nimrod was not just a king — he was a counterfeit messiah. The tower was not just a structure — it was a counterfeit mountain of God.

Thus, Babel marked the first **organised rebellion of stars**.

2. Astrological Rebellion — Counterfeit Constellations

- **Chronology**: From Eden to Babel, mankind moved eastward. First Adam eastward into Eden, then Cain eastward into Nod, now all nations eastward into Shinar. The East became the testing ground of light and darkness.

- **Typology**: God's true stars are Abraham's seed, promised to shine in heaven (Genesis 15:5). But Nimrod's stars sought to establish a counterfeit zodiac — the worship of created lights instead of the Creator. Astrology was born at Babel as man tried to replace the divine order of stars with his own reading of constellations.

- **Spiritology**: Every zodiac sign at Babel was an imitation of God's prophetic constellations. The Lamb was twisted into Aries, the Lion into Leo, the Virgin into Virgo. What was originally God's gospel in the heavens (Psalm 19) became distorted into idol worship.

- **Soulogy**: By gazing at the stars for guidance, man exchanged the inner witness of the Spirit for external signs. Their souls became enslaved to fate, and their destinies chained to counterfeit alignments.

Thus, Babel was the **first horoscope rebellion** — man reading his destiny from creation instead of Creator.

3. God Scatters the Eastward Rebellions

- **Theology**: God descended at Babel not just to confuse tongues, but to scatter counterfeit stars. Their unity was rebellion, their one language was witchcraft, their tower was pride, their eastward gaze was idolatry.

- **Spiritology**: The scattering was judgment, but also mercy. By confounding their tongues, God prevented the solidification of a global rebellion that would have birthed an early Antichrist system.

- **Chronology**: Out of this scattering, Abraham is called — also from the East (Ur of the Chaldees). Thus, God raises His own star from the same region where counterfeit stars rose. What Nimrod began, Abraham would overturn.

- **Technology**: The bricks of Babel were the first counterfeit technology. They said, "let us make brick, and burn them thoroughly" (*Genesis 11:3*). Bricks are man-made, uniform, lifeless — unlike God's living stones. This was the technology of conformity, a system where individuality and divine design were erased for human control.

Thus, Babel reveals the principle: **when man builds eastward without God, he rises into rebellion; but when God raises His stars eastward, they shine with glory.**

Prophetic Flow of Irathiro at Babel

- Babel is the **first counterfeit Irathiro** — a rising not of holy stars, but of rebellious ones.
- Babel birthed the systems of **Babylon, astrology, witchcraft, and idolatry**.

- Yet out of Babel's scattering, the true East Gate emerges — Abraham, the father of stars by faith.

Spoken Decree (Altar of the East Gate)

"O Lord of Hosts, scatter every counterfeit star, every false tower, every Babel that rises against Your throne. Let every false name be erased, and let the Name above all names be exalted. From Babel to Zion, let Irathiro rise in righteousness. Amen."

PART II

STARS OF THE PROMISE — ABRAHAM TO JOSEPH

CHAPTER 4

Abraham and the Covenant of Stars

Stars of the Promise — Abraham to Joseph

The Eastward Call of Abraham

When God called Abram out of Ur of the Chaldees, He was calling him out of the counterfeit constellations of Babylon. Ur was a land dominated by moon-worship, astrology, and the reading of false stars. Yet into this night sky, God spoke a different word:

> *"Look now toward heaven, and tell the stars, if thou be able to number them…" (Genesis 15:5).*

This was not a poetic metaphor. It was a prophetic transaction. God was sealing a covenant not only in Abraham's body (circumcision) but also in the heavens. The true eastward star-lineage was being planted.

The Mystery of the Covenant Stars

- **Spiritology**: Stars here represent spirits of destinies. Abraham's seed would be clothed in the Spirit of Light, rising as holy witnesses in the heavens. The Spirit of Promise sealed his descendants as "star-seeds," carriers of divine testimony.

- **Soulogy**: The soul of Abraham had to be detached from astrology and attached to faith. His gaze shifted from calculating constellations to believing the invisible Word. His imagination, once colonized by Babylon, was reborn as the womb of promise.

- **Physiology**: Circumcision in Abraham's flesh was the bodily seal of this covenant. The stars Abraham saw above were inscribed in his very body below — the eternal mark in his bloodline.

- **Theology**: God alone is the Maker of stars. By commanding Abraham to look at them, He declared sovereignty over all destinies, exposing astrology as a counterfeit system. The covenant stars were not merely astronomical but eschatological — pointing to Christ Himself, the Morning Star (***Revelation 22:16***).

Eastward Journeys of Abraham

Abraham journeyed eastward again and again:

- From Haran, he went east to the land of Canaan, following a divine compass.

- When Lot chose the plain of Jordan "eastward" (***Genesis 13:11***), Lot aligned with Sodom — the counterfeit east. Abraham remained in the covenant east.

- On Mount Moriah (in the east of Salem), Abraham lifted his eyes and saw the true Lamb.

The rhythm of Abraham's life was guided not by astrology but by covenant stars. Every eastward step was a courtroom witness: Abraham stood in the east gate of history as a prophetic father of nations.

True Star Lineage vs. Counterfeit Seed

- **Isaac, the star-child of promise**, was born not by the will of flesh but by the Spirit. His conception broke the barrenness of Sarah's womb and aligned Abraham's house with heavenly constellations of covenant.

- **Ishmael, the counterfeit star**, though blessed with multiplication, represented a different constellation — a rising of flesh and strife, not Spirit and promise. His seed became a wandering star-system, often in opposition to Isaac.

- **Jacob and Esau** further dramatised this star-war. Jacob, though flawed, aligned with the promise. Esau despised his birthright, selling his star inheritance for a bowl of red stew.

The Prophetic Flow of Covenant Stars

Abraham's covenant of stars was not just about numbers but about a prophetic genealogy:

- From Abraham would rise **a star-scepter** (*Numbers 24:17*).

- From Jacob would rise **twelve star-tribes**, constellations of governance and glory.

- From Joseph's dream would rise **the sun, the moon, and eleven stars** bowing — a heavenly courtroom vision of Israel's prophetic destiny.

Thus, the covenant of stars was the proto-gospel. Abraham's faith aligned with heaven's courtroom, binding earth to heaven through promise.

Seal of the Spirit of Judgment and Burning

The covenant stars demand judgment on counterfeit constellations. Every Babylonian astrology, every Islamic crescent, every occult zodiac is judged in light of Abraham's eastward gaze. The Spirit of Judgment and Burning (**Isaiah 4:4**) purges false lights and seals the true Morning Star in Christ.

Prophetic Activation — Abraham's Star Gaze

- Lift up your eyes tonight and declare: *"I renounce every counterfeit star of my bloodline. I align with the covenant stars of Abraham in Christ Jesus. I am born of promise, not of flesh. My destiny is sealed in the Morning Star."*

- Pray **Psalm 147:4**: *"He telleth the number of the stars; he calleth them all by their names."* Declare: *"My name is not lost in the zodiac. My name is called by God's own voice among His stars."*

Thus Abraham rises as the Father of Stars, and Irathiro — the East Gate — burns brighter with covenant promise.

CHAPTER 5

Jacob — The Gate of Stars

1. Jacob's Ladder at Bethel (Stars Ascending and Descending)

"And he dreamed, and behold a ladder set up on the earth, and the top of it reached to heaven: and behold the angels of God ascending and descending on it." (Genesis 28:12)

When Jacob fled from Esau, he laid his head upon a stone at Bethel and received a starry vision. The ladder was not a mere stairway — it was the East Gate reopened.

- **Spiritology**: The angels ascending and descending were **star-messengers**, carrying decrees from the heavenly courtroom into the earth. Bethel became a portal of Irathiro — a rising of holy traffic between dimensions.

- **Soulogy:** Jacob's soul, restless and fearful, was brought into encounter. His dream aligned his emotions with destiny — transforming his fear into awe. *"Surely the LORD is in this place; and I knew it not."* (**Gen. 28:16**).

- **Physiology**: His head rested on a stone — prophetic of Christ, the Cornerstone. The stone became an altar, binding Jacob's body to the covenant of promise.
- **Theology**: Bethel revealed that the **star-gate between heaven and earth is not astrology, but covenant**. Angels rise and descend not by zodiac charts but by the Word spoken from heaven.

Thus, Jacob at Bethel became the witness of a **constellation of traffic**, a star-gate that aligned earth with heaven.

2. Wrestling at Peniel — Transformation into Israel

At Peniel, Jacob wrestled with a Man till daybreak (*Genesis 32:24–30*). This was not mere wrestling — it was a **courtroom encounter in the East Gate at dawn**.

- **Spiritology**: The Man was a Christophany, the Bright and Morning Star Himself. Jacob wrestled not with flesh but with the Judge of stars.
- **Soulogy**: His soul, filled with deceit (Jacob = "supplanter"), was burned into truth. He moved from manipulation to brokenness, from self to surrender.
- **Physiology**: His thigh was touched — his walk was forever changed. From that day, Jacob bore the mark of star-transformation in his very body.
- **Theology**: He was renamed *Israel* — "a prince with God." This was not just a new name but a **new constellation**. Jacob ceased to be a wandering star; he became the father of a 12-star government (*Revelation 12:1*).

At Peniel, the East dawn rose upon Jacob. His wrestling birthed Israel, the star-constellation of God's covenant people.

3. Israel as God's Constellation

From Jacob's loins came **twelve tribes** — the true star-map of God's government.

- **Chronology**: Just as the heavens declare glory through constellations (**Psalm 19**), Israel was planted as a constellation in history — a prophetic sky upon the earth.

- **Typology**: The 12 tribes mirror the 12 signs of heaven, but purified. Where Babel twisted constellations into zodiac idolatry, Israel embodied them in covenant truth.

- **Technology**: The tabernacle of Moses later camped the tribes in a formation mirroring heavenly constellations — God's true astronomy. Every placement of tribe, banner, and stone on the high priest's breastplate was an alignment of heaven and earth.

Thus, Israel became God's **living constellation**, a nation shining as stars among the nations (**Daniel 12:3**).

4. The Gate of Stars in Prophetic Vision

- Jacob at Bethel opened the **vertical star-gate** (angels ascending and descending).

- Jacob at Peniel opened the **transformational star-gate** (man becoming Israel).

- Israel as 12 tribes opened the **governmental star-gate** (God's constellation of rulership).

The East Gate of Irathiro thus shifts from individual (Abraham) to corporate (Israel). The promise is no longer one star but a whole constellation rising.

Prophetic Sealing

- **Spiritology**: Jacob reveals the star-gate is Christ Himself, bridging heaven and earth.

- **Soulogy**: True star-witnesses are birthed through brokenness, not pride.

- **Physiology**: Our bodies become marked temples of transformation, like Jacob's thigh.

- **Theology**: Israel is not just a nation but a prophetic constellation, aligned to govern in the heavenly courtroom.

Activation Decree — The Gate of Stars

"I declare that I am aligned with the star-gate of Zion. Like Jacob at Bethel, I see angels ascending and descending upon Christ the Ladder. Like Israel at Peniel, I am transformed in the dawn of Irathiro. I belong not to wandering stars, but to God's constellation of covenant. Let my life shine as one star among the twelve in Zion's courtroom, forever sealed in the Light of the Morning Star."

CHAPTER 6

Joseph — The Dream of Sun, Moon, and Stars

The Courtroom of Egypt

1. The Prophetic Dream of Stars

"Behold, I have dreamed a dream more; and, behold, the sun and the moon and the eleven stars made obeisance to me." (Genesis 37:9)

Joseph's dream was not ordinary — it was **the court summons of destiny**. God unveiled to him the **prophetic order of stars**:

- **The Sun** — Jacob, the father, the governing authority.
- **The Moon** — Rachel (and Leah by extension), the reflective order of the mothers.
- **The Stars** — his eleven brothers, the constellation of Israel.

In Joseph's dream, he was lifted as the twelfth star — the star of rulership, clothed in authority, set apart to shine in Egypt.

- **Spiritology**: Joseph's spirit carried the light of governance, a mantle of star-authority to interpret dreams and rule kingdoms.

- **Soulogy**: Though rejected, betrayed, and broken, his soul was refined until it became the vessel of divine wisdom.

- **Physiology**: His body endured pits, prisons, and palaces — yet each became a courtroom stage where God's star-light in him could not be extinguished.

- **Theology**: Joseph's star pointed to Christ — despised, rejected, cast down, yet exalted to reign as the true Bright and Morning Star.

2. Egypt as the Stage of False and True Stars

Egypt was not a neutral ground. It was the **centre of counterfeit astronomy**. The pyramids were star-temples aligned to Orion and Sirius, designed as gateways for fallen star-worship. Pharaohs claimed to be sons of the sun-god Ra, binding destinies under the false east.

Into this stage of counterfeit constellations, Joseph rose as a **true east star**.

- **Chronology**: While Babel birthed astrology, Egypt perfected it in monuments and mysteries.

- **Typology**: Pharaoh's magicians, who claimed mastery of stars, were exposed by Joseph's Spirit-led interpretations. Their charts could not reveal what Joseph declared by the Spirit of God.

- **Technology**: Egypt used pyramids as **star-chambers**, but Joseph built storehouses of grain — true technology guided by revelation, not divination.

- **Theology**: Egypt was a courtroom where false stars were weighed against the true star. Joseph became the witness, exposing Egypt's false light and enthroning God's wisdom.

Thus Egypt became the stage where star-warfare was decided — and Joseph, the true star, prevailed.

3. Joseph as a Prophetic East Star

Irathiro means the rising of the sun, the place of first light. Joseph himself was such a star:

- He rose in the **East of Egypt** — from the pit of Dothan, to Potiphar's house, to Pharaoh's throne.

- He carried a **starry garment** — the coat of many colours, a prophetic mantle torn but not destroyed.

- He shone as a **light in famine** — while the nations were darkened by scarcity, his wisdom became their sunrise.

- He became the **saviour of Israel** — preserving the constellation of twelve tribes when famine threatened to extinguish them.

Joseph's rise was not just personal vindication — it was the **covenant rising of Irathiro**. He was the prophetic east star sent ahead to preserve Israel's constellation in a foreign courtroom.

4. The Courtroom of Egypt

Every stage of Joseph's life was a courtroom trial:

- **The Pit** — judgment by brothers, but God overruled.

- **Potiphar's House** — judgment by slander, but God preserved.

- **The Prison** — judgment of men, but dreams began to testify.

- **Pharaoh's Throne** — final courtroom, where Joseph's star shone, and God's verdict was sealed: *"Can we find such a one as this, a man in whom the Spirit of God is?"* (**Gen. 41:38**).

In Egypt's courtroom, Joseph's star broke through. He rose not by divination, but by the Spirit of the Living God.

5. Prophetic Meaning for Irathiro

Joseph shows us that:

- True stars shine not in ease but in trial.
- False stars may rise eastward, but God scatters them in judgment.
- The covenant star of Abraham must pass through pits, prisons, and palaces before it rules in glory.
- Christ Himself, the ultimate Joseph, would descend into rejection and rise as the Morning Star enthroned.

Joseph is Irathiro — a star rising out of the East, shining in Egypt, preserving Israel, and pointing to Christ.

Sealing Revelation

- **Spiritology**: Dreams are heavenly decrees — Joseph was clothed in the spirit of stars.
- **Soulogy**: His soul was purified until he could govern without vengeance.
- **Physiology**: His body carried the scars of pits and prisons, yet was enthroned in palace robes.
- **Theology**: Joseph fulfilled the star-prophecy of Abraham — his seed shining among nations, preserved by a star raised in

Egypt.

Prophetic Decree:
"I am a Joseph-star in the courtroom of Egypt. My dreams are not divinations but decrees of heaven. No pit, prison, or false accusation can dim my rising. I shine by the Spirit of God, not by astrology or human wisdom. I preserve nations in famine, I preserve the covenant constellation of Zion. I rise as a prophetic east star, sealed in Christ, the Bright and Morning Star."

PART III

PROPHETS OF THE EAST GATE

CHAPTER 7

Balaam and the Star of Jacob

The Clash of Holy and Sorcery Stars at the East Gate

1. The Prophecy of the Star of Jacob

> *"There shall come a Star out of Jacob, and a Sceptre shall rise out of Israel, and shall smite the corners of Moab, and destroy all the children of Sheth." (Numbers 24:17)*

Balaam, though hired to curse, was forced by God's Spirit to prophesy the rising of a true star. This star pointed to:

- **David**, the warrior-king who would subdue Moab.
- **Christ**, the Bright and Morning Star who would destroy the serpent-seed (Sheth).
- **Israel**, the nation shining as God's covenant constellation at the East Gate of Canaan.

This prophecy was not just about a distant Messiah — it was about **the courtroom clash of stars** right at the border of Moab.

- **Spiritology**: God spoke through Balaam's spirit though he was corrupted — proving that even false prophets must bow to divine decree.

- **Soulogy**: Balaam's divided soul — greedy for Moab's gold but caught in God's Word — reveals the warfare between desire and destiny.

- **Physiology**: His very donkey became a courtroom witness, showing that creation itself can testify when men resist truth.

- **Theology**: The Star of Jacob is Christ, whose light breaks through every sorcery altar and scatters the hosts of counterfeit stars.

2. The Battle of Holy Stars vs. Sorcery Stars

Moab was not merely a political enemy — it was a **spiritual gate of sorcery**. Balak, king of Moab, summoned Balaam to use enchantments, knowing that Israel was rising like a star-army.

- **Holy Stars**: Israel's tribes camped as a cross-shaped constellation (**Numbers 2**) — a prophetic mirror of the stars of heaven.

- **Sorcery Stars**: Moab's priests aligned with Balaam's divinations, trying to pull heavenly verdicts against Israel.

- **Courtroom of the East Gate**: Every altar built by Balaam was a counterfeit attempt to override God's decree with sorcery.

But in every trial, **the holy stars prevailed**. Balaam could only speak blessing, declaring: *"God hath blessed, and I cannot reverse it."* (**Numbers 23:20**).

- **Chronology**: Each sacrifice Balaam offered was timed to intercept Israel's march — yet each failed.

- **Typology**: Balaam represents all false prophets who try to manipulate the stars but end up testifying to the true Light.

- **Technology**: Moab used altars as "frequency stations" to summon powers of the East — but heaven overruled them.
- **Theology**: The holy star of Jacob stood immovable against counterfeit alignments.

3. Moabite Altars as Counterfeit East Gates

Balak built **seven altars, seven bulls, and seven rams** (*Numbers 23:1–4*), mimicking divine patterns. But these were **counterfeit east gates**:

- They faced eastward, toward the rising of the sun, but not toward God's covenant light.
- They invoked sorcery and enchantment instead of Spirit-led sacrifice.
- They sought to block Israel's entry into the Promised Land through spiritual manipulation.

Yet these altars collapsed in verdict. Instead of curses, they became pulpits of blessing. Every time Balaam opened his mouth, the East Gate declared Israel's destiny: *"How goodly are thy tents, O Jacob!"* (**Num. 24:5**).

Moab's counterfeit gate could not withstand the true East Star.

4. Prophetic Meaning for Irathiro

Balaam's encounter shows us that:

- The East Gate is always contested — holy stars vs. sorcery stars.
- False prophets may read stars, but only God writes them.
- The Star of Jacob is not subject to enchantment — it rises by

decree.

- Christ, the true Morning Star, shatters all Moabite altars and scatters every sorcery star.

For Irathiro, it means: the rising of God's true star in the East cannot be intercepted, even if sorcerers, false prophets, and counterfeit gates oppose it.

Sealing Revelation

- **Spiritology**: Even corrupt vessels must prophesy the truth when heaven decrees it.
- **Soulogy**: Greed and lust for reward blind men at the East Gate.
- **Physiology**: Creation itself testifies when man resists the true Word.
- **Theology**: The Star of Jacob is Christ — rising eastward to judge Moab and preserve Israel.

Prophetic Decree:

"I stand at the East Gate under the Star of Jacob. No enchantment, no sorcery, no counterfeit altar can reverse my blessing. I reject the counsel of Balaam and the rewards of Moab. My star rises eastward by decree, sealed in the covenant constellation of Christ, the Bright and Morning Star."

CHAPTER 8

Lucifer — The Fallen East Star

The Counterfeit Irathiro vs. the True Morning Star

1. How Art Thou Fallen, O Lucifer?

> "How art thou fallen from heaven, O Lucifer, son of the morning! How art thou cut down to the ground, which didst weaken the nations!" (Isaiah 14:12)

Isaiah gives us the most piercing vision of the fall of a star. Lucifer — helel ben-shachar in Hebrew — means shining one, son of dawn. He was once a bright east star, reflecting God's light, standing at the dawn of creation as a seed-bearer of glory.

But pride corrupted him. He sought not to reflect, but to **originate light**. His fall was not simply a slip — it was a courtroom rebellion. He declared:

- "I will ascend into heaven."

- "I will exalt my throne above the stars of God."

- *"I will sit also upon the mount of the congregation, in the sides of the north."*
- *"I will ascend above the heights of the clouds."*
- *"I will be like the Most High."*

This fivefold declaration was his counterfeit **Irathiro** — an attempt to create his own East Gate apart from God.

But heaven's verdict resounded: *"Yet thou shalt be brought down to hell, to the sides of the pit."* (**Isa. 14:15**).

2. Lucifer as Counterfeit Irathiro

Lucifer's rebellion reveals that every **false star** is a counterfeit *Irathiro*. Instead of rising by God's Word, it rises by ambition, sorcery, and deception.

- **Spiritology**: Lucifer twisted his spirit from reflection to rebellion. He no longer bore light; he tried to generate it.
- **Soulogy**: His will became a throne of pride, turning eastward glory into self-worship.
- **Physiology**: His very form, once covered with stones of fire (**Ezekiel 28:13–14**), became corrupted, his brightness darkened.
- **Theology**: Lucifer became the prototype of every false morning star — claiming dawn but bringing night.

Lucifer tried to stand as Irathiro — the first light — but became the first counterfeit.

3. The Clash of Morning Stars: Lucifer vs. Christ

The Scriptures draw a deliberate **contrast of stars**:

- **Lucifer, son of the morning (*Isa. 14:12*)** — a fallen star, now a dragon, cast to earth.

- **Christ, the Bright and Morning Star (*Rev. 22:16*)** — the eternal star, faithful and true, who rises at the end to usher the everlasting dawn.

This is not mere poetry — it is the **courtroom contest of stars**:

- **Lucifer**: Sought to ascend, to steal God's throne, and to counterfeit eastward glory.
- **Christ**: Humbled Himself, descended to the grave, and was exalted to the highest throne.

Lucifer wanted to be like God. Christ *was* God, but chose to become man — and was crowned with glory. This reversal is the verdict: **the false morning star falls, the true Morning Star rises.**

4. The Judgment of the Fallen East Star

Lucifer's judgment was cosmic:

- He was **cast down like lightning (*Luke 10:18*)**.
- His tail drew **a third of the stars of heaven (*Rev. 12:4*)** — angels who joined his rebellion.
- He was stripped of glory, becoming Satan, the accuser.
- His destiny is the **pit and the lake of fire** — the final east gate of judgment.
- **Chronology**: His fall marks the first courtroom trial in heaven — the rebellion of the star-bearer.
- **Typology**: Every false leader who claims light without God repeats Lucifer's pattern.
- **Technology**: His use of music, stones, and trading in Eden (*Ezek. 28*) became the instruments of sorcery and

counterfeit worship.

- **Theology**: His counterfeit Irathiro is doomed to collapse.

5. Christ — The True Morning Star

Against Lucifer's fall stands Christ's eternal rise:

- *"I am the root and the offspring of David, and the bright and morning star."* (**Rev. 22:16**)
- *"The day star arise in your hearts."* (**2 Peter 1:19**)

Where Lucifer fell eastward, Christ rises eastward:

- **Spiritology**: He is the eternal Word, the true Light that lights every man (*John 1:9*).
- **Soulogy**: He obeyed unto death, and was exalted far above every name.
- **Physiology**: His transfigured body shone brighter than the sun (*Matt. 17:2*).
- **Theology**: Christ is the uncreated Irathiro — the dawn of the new creation.

Thus the courtroom decree is sealed: the counterfeit morning star falls, but the true Morning Star rises forever.

Sealing Revelation

- Lucifer was the counterfeit Irathiro — fallen east star.
- His rebellion birthed wandering stars, false lights, and counterfeit dawns.
- Christ alone is the true Irathiro, the Bright and Morning Star.
- The East Gate belongs to Him — and to the remnant who rise in His light.

Prophetic Decree:

"I reject every counterfeit Irathiro. I renounce the pride of Lucifer and every false morning star. I align with the Bright and Morning Star, Jesus Christ. I rise with Him at the East Gate, clothed with true light, sealed in Zion, shining forever as a star in His constellation."

CHAPTER 9

Ezekiel's East Gate of Glory

The Throne, the River, and the Rising of Zion

1. The Glory Entering from the East

> "And behold, the glory of the God of Israel came from the way of the east: and his voice was like a noise of many waters: and the earth shined with his glory." (Ezekiel 43:2)

Ezekiel saw it: the Shekinah Glory, which had once departed (Ezek. 10–11), now returning. And where did it come from? The East.

This is Irathiro in its purest form — the true light of God's presence entering through the East Gate of the temple.

- **Spiritology**: The Spirit of Glory moves eastward, showing us the divine order of rising.
- **Soulogy**: Israel's heart, once broken and exiled, would be

healed by the returning glory.

- **Physiology**: The temple itself — the body of the nation — becomes radiant as the glory enters.
- **Theology**: The East Gate belongs to the King of Glory; no man can shut it once He enters.

The sound was **like many waters**, echoing *Revelation 1:15* — the voice of Christ. Ezekiel was not just seeing the return from Babylon — he was seeing the prophetic *Irathiro* of Messiah's reign.

2. The River Flowing Eastward

> *"Afterward he brought me again unto the door of the house; and behold, waters issued out from under the threshold of the house eastward..." (Ezekiel 47:1)*

From the same temple came **a river of life**, flowing eastward, growing deeper with every measure.

This is not coincidence — the **glory enters eastward**, and the **river flows eastward**. Glory and river are inseparable. Where the King enters, life flows.

- **Chronology**: The river begins at ankle depth, then knee, then loins, then becomes a river too deep to pass — showing the increasing measure of Spirit.
- **Typology**: This river is Christ's Spirit, the living water, flowing into the barren east (toward the Dead Sea) and transforming death into life.
- **Technology**: The temple is the "fountainhead" — showing that the body of Christ becomes the channel of the Spirit's eastward flow.

- **Theology**: Irathiro is not just light — it is also living water. The East Gate births the stream of eternal life.

Everywhere the river flowed, healing came. Even the salty waters of the Dead Sea were healed — a prophecy that the nations eastward, barren under false stars, would be revived by the true river.

3. The Restoration of Zion as Eastward Throne

Ezekiel's vision culminates in a declaration:
"*And the name of the city from that day shall be, The LORD is there (YHWH Shammah).*" (***Ezekiel 48:35***)

The East Gate is not just about entry — it is about **enthronement**. The glory that entered becomes permanent, and the river that flowed becomes eternal. Zion is restored as God's throne, facing eastward.

- **Spiritology**: Zion's spirit is re-lit with the morning of God's presence.
- **Soulogy**: The exile of the soul is reversed; the people are gathered back to the covenant.
- **Physiology**: The land itself is healed; the desert blossoms; the trees bear fruit each month.
- **Theology**: The East Gate is sealed for the Prince (***Ezek. 44:1–2***) — Christ Himself, the true Irathiro, who alone may enter.

Thus, the East Gate becomes the cosmic courtroom of glory: judgment for false stars, but restoration and enthronement for Zion.

Sealing Revelation

- The **glory** of God always rises eastward — the sign of divine return.

- The **river** of God always flows eastward — the life-stream of Spirit.

- The **throne** of God is established eastward — Zion as the city where the LORD dwells.

- The East Gate is not just history — it is prophecy. Christ, the true Prince, has entered it, and His Spirit still flows from it.

Prophetic Decree:
"I align with the East Gate of Glory. Let the King of Glory enter into my temple. Let His river flow eastward from my spirit, healing all barren places. I declare Zion restored, enthroned as Irathiro — the rising of the LORD's glory in the earth."

CHAPTER 10

Daniel — Stars in Judgment

The Courtroom of Falling and Rising Lights

1. The Horn that Cast Down the Stars (Daniel 8)

> "And it waxed great, even to the host of heaven; and it cast down some of the host and of the stars to the ground, and stamped upon them." (Daniel 8:10)

Daniel saw a little horn that grew arrogant, challenging heaven itself. This horn trampled the stars of God — a prophetic picture of persecution against the righteous and angelic hosts.

- **Spiritology**: The horn represents rebellious spirit-powers that rise eastward but without covenant light.
- **Soulogy**: Nations and rulers driven by pride, like Antiochus and later Antichrist, wage war against the stars of truth.
- **Physiology**: Saints, persecuted in body, are symbolised as stars stamped down — yet their blood cries out as

testimony.

- **Theology**: No horn can extinguish the true Irathiro. Though stars fall, the Bright and Morning Star rises above all.

This vision reveals the **courtroom tension** of Irathiro: the false horn rises, but only for a season. Judgment was decreed — "unto two thousand and three hundred days; then shall the sanctuary be cleansed." (***Dan. 8:14***). Even the fall of stars is measured under God's verdict.

2. The Righteous Shine as Stars (*Daniel 12:3*)

> *"And they that be wise shall shine as the brightness of the firmament; and they that turn many to righteousness as the stars for ever and ever."*

Here is Daniel's verdict of Irathiro: **true stars cannot be destroyed**. They shine forever, sealed in righteousness.

- **Spiritology**: Wisdom (the Spirit of counsel and might) clothes the righteous with star-glory.
- **Soulogy**: Those who turn others to righteousness radiate light from their very souls.
- **Physiology**: In resurrection, the righteous bodies will shine like stars (cf. ***1 Cor. 15:41–42***).
- **Theology**: The star-constellation of God's people is eternal; no horn, no dragon, no false east can erase them.

Thus Irathiro is not just about one star — it is about a **constellation of the remnant**, shining together in the firmament of Zion.

3. Prophetic Warfare: Angels vs. Stars of Darkness

Daniel also unveils the **angelic courtroom battles** behind the stars:

- In *Daniel 10*, the angel Gabriel speaks of **the prince of Persia** resisting him — a dark principality over an eastern gate.
- Michael, the archangel, rises as the star-warrior for Israel.
- Daniel himself, fasting and praying, becomes part of the star-war, drawing heaven's verdict on earth.

This shows that **Irathiro is a battlefield of stars and angels**:

- Holy angels as morning stars, aligned with God's throne.
- Dark powers as fallen stars, resisting the eastward rising of glory.
- The saints, shining as righteous stars, caught in between yet destined to overcome.

Sealing Revelation

- *Daniel 8*: False horns trample stars, but only within God's measured season.
- *Daniel 12*: True stars — the wise and righteous — shine forever, clothed in eternal light.
- Angelic warfare at the East Gate reveals that the rising of stars is a courtroom conflict in the heavens.
- Irathiro is sealed: no matter how many stars fall, the righteous constellation will shine in Zion eternally.

Prophetic Decree:
"I rise as a star of righteousness in the courtroom of Irathiro. No horn shall trample my light, no power of darkness shall extinguish my flame. I join the constellation of the remnant,

clothed in wisdom, sealed in glory, aligned with Michael and the armies of heaven. I shall shine as a star forever in Zion."

CHAPTER 11

Bethlehem — The Star of the East

Christ the True Irathiro

1. Wise Men from the East — True Irathiro Witnesses

> "Where is he that is born King of the Jews? for we have seen his star in the east, and are come to worship him." (Matthew 2:2)

From the lands eastward came wise men — magoi, star-watchers. Yet these were not sorcerers like Balaam; they were righteous seekers who discerned the true star of promise.

- They fulfilled Daniel's prophecy (**Dan. 12:3**), shining as those who turned many to righteousness.
- They were the **first Gentile witnesses** of Irathiro — proving that the rising star was not only for Israel but for the nations.

- Their journey was an **eastward testimony**: stars rising in the nations now bowing to the true Morning Star in Bethlehem.

Spiritology: Their spirits were drawn not by astrology, but by the decree of heaven.
Soulogy: Their desire was not conquest but worship, aligning their hearts with the King.
Physiology: They travelled with gold, frankincense, and myrrh — prophetic offerings of wealth, worship, and sacrifice; and also foretelling His trial, His suffering, and His death — that through His wounds, every nation's healing would begin.
Theology: Their arrival announced the end of counterfeit Irathiro. A new dawn had come.

The wise men were the **first fruits of the nations**, entering the East Gate to acknowledge the true Star.

2. The Bethlehem Star — Heaven Testifying to the King

The star they saw was no ordinary constellation. It was heaven's courtroom verdict: **the King has been born.**

- *Genesis 1:14* — Stars were set "for signs and for seasons." Bethlehem's star was such a sign.

- *Numbers 24:17* — Balaam's prophecy: *"There shall come a Star out of Jacob."* Now fulfilled.

- *Isaiah 9:2* — *"The people that walked in darkness have seen a great light."*

The Bethlehem Star was the convergence of all prophecy:

- The true light rising eastward.

- The testimony of heaven that Christ is the Irathiro.

- The sign to both Israel and the nations that the Morning Star had broken the night.

This star stood still over Bethlehem, showing that **Irathiro is not wandering**. Unlike Lucifer's fallen stars, Christ's light is stable, unwavering, fixed by decree.

Chronology: At the appointed time, the star appeared.
Typology: Bethlehem (house of bread) birthed the Star of Life.
Technology: The star itself functioned as God's divine navigation — a spiritual GPS guiding men to Christ.
Theology: The true Irathiro is both King and Lamb, both star and bread.

3. War with Herod's Counterfeit Star System

When true Irathiro rises, counterfeit stars always manifest. Herod, a puppet-king under Rome, immediately felt threatened.

- **Herod's star system** was political power, rooted in fear and bloodshed.
- He sought to kill the newborn King, proving that counterfeit Irathiro always wars against true light.
- The massacre of infants in Bethlehem echoed Pharaoh's slaughter — the dragon waiting to devour the child (***Rev. 12:4***).

But heaven overruled:

- The wise men were warned in a dream.
- Joseph, the star-father, was guided to Egypt.
- The child was preserved, for the decree of Irathiro cannot be reversed.

Thus the Bethlehem Star clashed with Herod's counterfeit system — and prevailed.

4. The Fulfillment of Daniel's Vision

Daniel foresaw stars trampled, but also stars shining forever. In Bethlehem, the prophecy converged:

- Christ, the Bright and Morning Star, rose unchallenged.
- Wise men, righteous stars, were drawn to His light.
- Herod, the false horn, raged — but failed.

The Bethlehem Star is the **bridge from Daniel's courtroom to Revelation's throne**. The day star had arisen in history, and the nations had begun to see His light.

Sealing Revelation

- Wise men from the East are prophetic Irathiro witnesses — stars bowing to the Star.
- The Bethlehem Star is heaven's decree — Christ, the Bright and Morning Star, is born.
- Herod's counterfeit system is judged — no power can extinguish Irathiro.
- Daniel's vision finds fulfillment: the righteous shine with Him forever.

Prophetic Decree:
"I align with the Bethlehem Star, the true Irathiro. I renounce every Herodian counterfeit, every false throne, every power that seeks to extinguish the Light. I follow the true Star, Jesus Christ, and I bow in worship with the wise men of the East. My rising is in Him, and my light shall never be quenched."

CHAPTER 12

Christ — The Bright and Morning Star

Irathiro Manifest in Flesh

1. *Revelation 22:16* — Christ as the Eternal East Star

"I Jesus have sent mine angel to testify unto you these things in the churches. I am the root and the offspring of David, and the bright and morning star." (Revelation 22:16)

t the close of Scripture, Christ unveils His eternal identity: the Bright and Morning Star.
- He is not a borrowed light like the moon, nor a fading constellation like fallen angels.
- He is **the source-light** — the eternal East Star, rising not from creation but from eternity itself.
- As *Root and Offspring of David*, He ties earth's throne to heaven's throne.

53

- As *Morning Star*, He declares the end of the long night of rebellion.

The Bright Star is both **beginning and end**:

- Beginning, because His rising initiates the new day.
- End, because His light judges and extinguishes the night forever.

Spiritology: His Spirit is light itself — the radiance of God's eternal being.
Soulogy: His will is unwavering; He is no wandering star, but fixed in perfect obedience.
Physiology: His very body became the vessel of glory, light shining through flesh.
Theology: He is Irathiro eternal — the East Gate fulfilled, the Light of the World.

2. The Transfiguration — Glory Shining Like the Sun

> "His face did shine as the sun, and his raiment was white as the light." (Matthew 17:2)

On the mountain, Christ unveiled the Irathiro glory hidden in flesh. Before Peter, James, and John:

- His face shone like the sun — declaring Him the true Day Star.
- His garments gleamed white — showing that even His covering was light.
- Moses (Law) and Elijah (Prophets) appeared, testifying that all the Word converges in Him.

This was not borrowed brilliance; it was **the eternal morning breaking forth**. The disciples saw what Lucifer sought falsely —

true radiance, not stolen but begotten.

Typology: The Mount of Transfiguration was the new Mount Sinai, but instead of thunder and darkness, the new covenant revealed light and grace.
Chronology: It occurred before the cross, as a preview of resurrection dawn.
Technology: Heaven's light frequency broke through mortal sight, calibrating the disciples to the true Irathiro.

At the Transfiguration, the East Star announced: the **veil of night is lifting**.

3. Resurrection — The Rising of the Eternal Light

> "But unto you that fear my name shall the Sun of righteousness arise with healing in his wings." (Malachi 4:2)

The resurrection was the true dawn. Christ, the Irathiro, rose from the grave not as a fading star but as the **eternal Light that death cannot quench.**

- **Eden's East Gate was closed by cherubim**, but now the gate is opened in Christ.
- The stone rolled away was not just an entrance to a tomb — it was the unveiling of the East Star rising.
- Death is darkness, but resurrection is the eternal day.

Spiritology: His Spirit broke the power of the grave.
Soulogy: His will endured unto obedience even in death, reversing Adam's fall.
Physiology: His body transformed into incorruptible glory, radiating eternal light.
Theology: Resurrection is the courtroom verdict — Irathiro

reigns, night is over.

The women came at dawn to the tomb but found the true dawn standing alive. The angel testified: *"He is not here, He is risen."* The Morning Star had risen, and with Him a new creation.

Sealing Revelation

- Christ is the **Bright and Morning Star** — eternal, unquenchable, and true.
- In the Transfiguration, His hidden glory burst forth as Irathiro before witnesses.
- In the Resurrection, He rose as the eternal dawn, the Sun of Righteousness.
- Night has ended; the East Gate is open; Irathiro reigns forever.

Prophetic Decree:

"I arise with Christ, the Bright and Morning Star. His light is my light; His glory is my rising. I renounce every false illumination, every wandering star, every counterfeit brightness. The dawn of Irathiro shines in me, and I shall shine forever with Him, for He is risen and reigns without end."

PART V

THE STARS OF THE CHURCH

CHAPTER 13

The Seven Stars in His Right Hand

The Church as Irathiro Carriers

1. *Revelation 1:20* **— Stars as Angel-Messengers**

> "The mystery of the seven stars which thou sawest in my right hand, and the seven golden candlesticks. The seven stars are the angels of the seven churches: and the seven candlesticks which thou sawest are the seven churches."

In John's vision, the resurrected Christ walks among the lampstands, clothed in priestly glory. His right hand holds seven stars — the angels or messengers of the churches.
This image is profound:

- The **lampstands** are the churches — bearers of earthly light.

- The **stars** are the angelic messengers — heavenly witnesses.

- Christ holds both — the entire order of worship and testimony — in His hand of power.

Spiritology: The Spirit unites heavenly stars and earthly lamps as one testimony of light.

Soulogy: The will of the Church must align with the will of heaven — otherwise lamps burn dim.

Physiology: Believers are earthen vessels, but they carry a starlight within that shines in darkness.

Theology: The sevenfold structure reflects the **Sabbath cycle** of perfection; the Church is ordered by the rhythm of heaven's Irathiro.

Thus, the Church is not random; it is a **constellation formed in Christ's hand.**

2. The Lampstands and Stars — Prophetic Alignment

The lampstands are rooted on earth, but the stars are positioned in heaven. Together, they reveal a mystery: **true witness is only complete when earth and heaven align.**

- If the lamp burns without a star, it is man-made religion without heaven's authority.
- If the star shines without lamp, it is angelic brilliance without earthly witness.
- Only when star and lamp agree, held together in Christ's right hand, is true Irathiro established.

This is why Christ walks among the lampstands to inspect alignment. He commends those burning with love and rebukes those whose light has grown dim. The churches become constellations, positioned eastward in the Spirit, carrying heaven's testimony on earth.

Typology: Just as Abraham looked at the stars for a covenant promise, now the Church is that living constellation, held in Christ's palm.

Chronology: This vision opens Revelation, because the end cannot be read without knowing who truly carries the stars of witness.

Technology: The "stars" are not physical; they are spiritual coordinates of authority, shining as signals in the unseen realm.

3. Warning Against Losing Star-Light

To the church at Ephesus, Christ warns: *"I will remove thy candlestick out of his place, except thou repent."* (**Revelation 2:5**).

This reveals a terrifying truth: **a star can be lost.**

- Not by fading like a natural star, but by being removed from divine alignment.
- A church that loses love, holiness, or faithfulness loses its lampstand and with it, its star-messenger.

Jude warns of *"wandering stars, to whom is reserved the blackness of darkness for ever."* (**Jude 1:13**). These are false lights, detached from Christ's hand, cast adrift into judgment.

The call of Irathiro to the Church is this: **remain in His hand, or be cast into darkness.**

- **Remain in love** — for only love keeps the lamp burning.
- **Remain in truth** — for only truth fixes the star in place.
- **Remain in Sabbath rest** — for only rest seals the Church as God's dwelling of light.

Sealing Revelation

- The Church is not just people; it is a constellation held in Christ's right hand.
- The seven stars = angelic witnesses; the seven lampstands = earthly churches; together they shine Irathiro.

- Without alignment, light is lost. Without love, lamps go out. Without Christ's hand, stars fall.
- The true Church is a starry Bride, ordered by heaven, burning on earth, sealed in Christ.

Prophetic Decree:
"I belong to the constellation of Christ. I shall not be a wandering star. My light will not go out. I align with the heavenly star-messengers, and my lamp burns in the oil of the Spirit. Held in His right hand, I shine as Irathiro, a witness of the true Light until He comes."

CHAPTER 14

Shining as Stars in a Crooked World

The East-to-West Witness of Irathiro

1. *Philippians 2:15* — Believers as Stars

> "…that ye may be blameless and harmless, the sons of God, without rebuke, in the midst of a crooked and perverse nation, among whom ye shine as lights [stars] in the world."

Paul sees the Church not merely as an assembly, but as a heavenly constellation set against the night sky of corruption.

- **Blameless**: purity is the fuel of star-light.
- **Harmless**: meekness is the posture of true light.
- **Sons of God**: identity is the root of radiance.
- **In the midst**: stars are not removed from night — they shine within it.

Spiritology: The Spirit empowers holiness that separates the believer from the darkness while still shining in it.
Soulogy: The mind renewed in Christ reflects His brightness, uncorrupted by perverse thought-patterns.
Physiology: Even the body becomes a lamp — a living temple radiating holiness.
Theology: The Church is positioned by God as His Irathiro in a world collapsing into night.

Thus, every believer becomes a **personal east star**, rising in the darkness of their generation.

2. Paul as a Star Rising to the Nations

Paul himself is a living Irathiro. Once a persecutor lost in night, he was struck by the Light on the road to Damascus. From that day, he rose as a star to the Gentiles.

- In **Philippi**, his imprisonment became a platform for light.
- In **Athens**, he confronted the counterfeit constellations of philosophy.
- In **Corinth**, his weakness displayed God's true power.
- In **Rome**, his chains became beams of the gospel.

He embodies the prophecy of *Isaiah 49:6*: *"I will also give thee for a light to the Gentiles, that thou mayest be my salvation unto the end of the earth."*

Paul's journey is an Irathiro arc — a star rising eastward in Jerusalem and shining westward across the Mediterranean world.

3. The East-to-West Movement of the Gospel

The gospel itself is a **star-movement** — it flows like Irathiro, from East to West, from first light to the nations.

- **Eden**: planted eastward (*Genesis 2:8*).
- **Bethlehem**: the East star rose at Christ's birth (*Matthew 2:2*).
- **Pentecost**: fire fell in Jerusalem, then spread outward.
- **Paul's mission**: carried the Light westward into Europe.
- **Our day**: the gospel circles the globe, preparing for the ultimate Irathiro — the Second Coming.

This movement reveals divine protocol: **God always begins in the East, but His light is destined to cover the earth.**

Chronology: The eastward planting always precedes global spread.
Typology: Just as the sun rises in the East and moves westward, so does the witness of Christ.
Technology: The Spirit carries the Word across cultures and languages, like light refracting through nations.

Thus, the gospel is not stagnant but rising — a dawn that will culminate in **the Day of the Lord.**

Sealing Revelation

- Believers are **stars shining in a crooked world** — purity is their radiance, identity their anchor.
- Paul rose as a prophetic star to the Gentiles, embodying the east-to-west arc of Irathiro.
- The gospel moves like the sun: rising in the East, shining to the West, destined to cover the whole earth.

Prophetic Decree:
"I shine as a star in this generation. I shall not blend into the darkness, but radiate Christ in the midst of a crooked world. I walk in Paul's testimony, a rising star to the nations. The Irathiro

movement flows through me: from East to West, from Zion to the ends of the earth, until the knowledge of the glory of the Lord fills all nations as the waters cover the sea."

PART VI

THE LAST DAYS — RISING AND FALLING STARS

CHAPTER 15

Signs in the Heavens

The Courtroom of Falling and Rising Stars

1. *Matthew 24:29* — Stars Falling from Heaven

> "Immediately after the tribulation of those days shall the sun be darkened, and the moon shall not give her light, and the stars shall fall from heaven, and the powers of the heavens shall be shaken."

Jesus anchors His prophecy of the end in heavenly signs.
- The **sun darkened** — the great light hidden.
- The **moon dimmed** — reflected light silenced.
- The **stars falling** — powers once exalted, now cast down.

This is not mere astronomy; it is **prophetic courtroom language.**
- Stars = rulers, authorities, and spiritual powers.

- Their falling = divine judgment and displacement.
- Their shaking = heaven itself preparing for a new order.

Spiritology: The Spirit testifies through heavenly order; when stars fall, it signals angelic and human thrones losing authority.
Soulogy: Souls tied to counterfeit stars will be shaken, wandering in darkness.
Physiology: Even creation itself groans — earthquakes, cosmic shifts, signs in sun and moon.
Theology: God announces judgment not only on earth, but in the heavens, for the court is universal.

Thus, *Matthew 24:29* is a **court summons** — the stars themselves are witnesses of coming judgment.

2. *Revelation 6:13* — **Stars Shaken**

> *"And the stars of heaven fell unto the earth, even as a fig tree casteth her untimely figs, when she is shaken of a mighty wind."*

John's vision deepens the same mystery. The stars fall **like unripe fruit shaken violently.**

- This points to **premature exposure** — counterfeit powers revealed before their time.
- The **mighty wind** is not random — it is the Spirit of Judgment blowing from the East.
- The **fig tree** recalls Israel's prophetic destiny — both true and false branches shaken before the end.

Here, Revelation unveils the great sifting:

- **Holy stars** are fixed in Christ's hand, shining brighter in darkness.

- **False stars** are cast down, stripped of covering, judged as wandering lights.

Typology: Just as Lucifer fell from heaven like lightning, so all counterfeit stars must fall.
Chronology: This shaking precedes the unveiling of the Lamb's sealed ones — a preparation for true Irathiro glory.
Technology: Heaven itself functions like a prophetic scroll; the falling of stars is a spiritual signal, decoded by those aligned with the Spirit.

3. Spiritual Technology of Heavenly Signs

Why does God use stars, sun, and moon as signs? Because they are **the first language of prophecy.**

> "And God said, Let there be lights in the firmament of the heaven... and let them be for signs, and for seasons, and for days, and years." (Genesis 1:14).

The **technology of heavenly signs** is built into creation:

- **Stars** = prophetic messengers, rulers, destinies.
- **Sun** = Christ's central authority and light.
- **Moon** = the Church reflecting His glory.
- **Eclipses, shakings, and fallings** = divine verdicts enacted in the courtroom of heaven.

Counterfeit astrology twists this technology into rebellion, but true Irathiro wisdom decodes them by the Spirit, not divination.

Spiritology: The Spirit is the interpreter of heavenly technology. Without Him, men wander into sorcery.
Soulogy: The mind renewed discerns the difference between God's sign and Satan's counterfeit.
Physiology: Even the human body follows heavenly order — circadian rhythms, times, and seasons testify.
Theology: Every falling star is not random — it is a courtroom decree manifesting in creation.

Thus, in the Last Days, as signs multiply, the question is not *"What is happening in the sky?"* but *"What verdict is heaven declaring?"*

Sealing Revelation

- Stars falling = thrones and powers being judged.
- Stars shaken = counterfeit lights exposed before time.
- Heavenly signs are spiritual technology, designed from Genesis to announce courtroom verdicts.
- Only by Irathiro wisdom can the Church discern between true and false signals.

Prophetic Decree:

"I will not be deceived by counterfeit constellations. I discern the courtroom verdicts of heaven. Though stars fall and heavens shake, I remain fixed in Christ, the Bright and Morning Star. The Spirit gives me Irathiro sight, and I read the heavens as God's scroll, not man's sorcery."

CHAPTER 16

The Dragon and the Falling Stars

1 The Dragon Sweeping a Third of the Stars

A great sign appears in heaven — a woman clothed with the sun, the moon beneath her feet, and upon her head a crown of twelve stars. But behold, another sign rises: the red dragon, full of fury and rebellion, with seven heads and ten horns. With his tail, he sweeps down a third of the stars of heaven, casting them to the earth.

This is the great cosmic rebellion — the counterfeit constellation of the serpent seeking to devour the seed of the woman before it is born. Stars that were ordained to shine in God's court are dragged into the dragon's constellation of darkness. The courtroom of heaven trembles with the accusation: who will stand, and who will fall?

2 War of Constellations — Holy vs. Unholy Armies

The heavens are no longer silent. Michael and his angels rise as a holy constellation of war, clashing with the dragon and his stars. Here, the battle is not merely of light against darkness, but of order against rebellion, of Irathiro against counterfeit eastward rising.

The righteous stars, aligned with the throne of God, stand in their brightness. The fallen stars, seduced by the dragon's tail, lose their place in heaven. What was once glorious is darkened, what was once luminous becomes corrupt. Yet in the clash, prophecy unfolds — the true seed is preserved, the child is caught up to God's throne, and Zion is established as the eastward gate of victory.

3 Binding of Fallen Stars

The dragon is cast down — not by his own will, but by the decree of heaven's court. His fallen stars are chained in darkness, bound until the day of judgment. Their false light, once masquerading as brilliance, is extinguished under the authority of Christ, the Bright and Morning Star.

Here is the mystery: fallen stars are not annihilated immediately, but held in a suspended darkness, waiting for the fire of judgment. They become wandering stars (*Jude 1:13*), destined for the blackness of eternal night.
But the faithful shine ever brighter, sealed in the constellation of Zion, the Irathiro of God. The dragon's sweeping tail may have deceived a third, but the remnant — sealed and appointed — remain as pillars of the eternal heavens.

Prophetic Key of Irathiro:
Every star is summoned to a constellation. The question is: will you be swept by the dragon's tail into rebellion, or will you rise eastward in the constellation of Christ, the Morning Star?

CHAPTER 17

Trumpets and Woes — Demonic Stars Released

1 Stars as Judgments — Revelation 8–9

When the trumpets sound, the heavens themselves become the courtroom of judgment. A great star falls from heaven, burning like a lamp, striking the rivers and fountains of waters — its name is Wormwood, and it poisons the nations. Another star is given the key to the bottomless pit, and when it opens, smoke rises as the breath of hell, darkening sun and air.

These are no ordinary stars, but personified judgments — angelic beings turned instruments of wrath. Heaven decrees their release, and the earth trembles beneath their sting.

2 Abaddon, Apollyon, and Hell's Eastward Release

From the abyss come locusts, crowned like false kings, faces of men but hearts of torment. Their king is the angel of the bottomless pit — Abaddon in Hebrew, Apollyon in Greek — "the Destroyer."

This is hell's eastward rising, a counterfeit Irathiro. Just as Christ rises as the Morning Star to give life, Apollyon rises as a star of destruction to devour. His army moves east to west, imitating the movement of true prophecy, but leaving only smoke and torment in its path.

The trumpet woes reveal that when stars fall, they become gateways. The fallen star with the abyss-key unlocks realms of torment, opening the counterfeit east gate of hell itself.

3 Counterfeit "Morning Stars" vs. Christ's Star

The fallen stars declare themselves as light-bearers, imitating the songs of the morning stars that once sang at creation (***Job 38:7***). But now their song is dissonance, their brilliance is darkness, their eastward rising is counterfeit glory.

Christ, the true Bright and Morning Star (***Revelation 22:16***), stands in contrast. Where the counterfeit stars rise to torment, Christ rises to heal. Where the abyss-star releases scorpions and locusts, Christ releases rivers of living water. Where Apollyon seeks to destroy, Christ gives eternal life.

The clash of stars is no longer distant prophecy, it becomes an immediate judgment. Trumpets sound, stars fall, and the world must choose: align with the Morning Star of Christ, or be swept into the blackened constellation of Abaddon.

Prophetic Key of Irathiro:

Every trumpet unveils the reality of spiritual constellations. Stars are not neutral, they are either sealed in Christ's constellation of life or released as instruments of destruction. The true eastward rising belongs to the Lamb; all other risings are counterfeit shadows of judgment.

CHAPTER 18

The Bright Morning Star Returns

1 *Revelation 22:16* — Final Revelation of the True Star

At the very end of Scripture, after seals, trumpets, bowls, and wars of stars, the voice of Christ declares with final authority:

> *"I Jesus… am the Root and the Offspring of David, and the Bright and Morning Star."*

Here, the Irathiro is sealed. No more counterfeits, no more imitations. The star that rose over Bethlehem now shines as the eternal Light of the New Creation. The Bright Morning Star is not simply an astronomical sign; He is the embodiment of God's first command — "Let there be light." He is the Alpha rising as the Omega, the First Light returning as the Last Light.

In this final revelation, Christ does not merely rise in the east; He *is* the East — the source of all beginnings and the gate of all glory.

2 New Jerusalem as the Eternal East Gate

John sees the city descending out of heaven, clothed with the brilliance of jewels, its foundations shining with the twelve tribal stones, its gates named after Israel. But note the prophetic order: **the city has no need of the sun or moon, for the Lamb is the Light thereof.** The New Jerusalem is the eternal Irathiro — the place where no counterfeit stars can rise, for the Lamb Himself is the eternal Morning.

The gates are never shut. Why? Because the East Gate has found its fullness in Christ. Ezekiel's vision of the glory entering from the east (*Ezekiel 43:2*) now becomes permanent. The city itself is the courtroom of light, the dwelling of righteous stars.

Here, all promises to Abraham are fulfilled, his seed shines as innumerable stars, gathered in the constellation of the Lamb. Joseph's dream is realised, Jacob's ladder is complete, Daniel's righteous ones now shine forever. Every star-war of Genesis to Revelation is resolved in the holy constellation of Zion.

3 Zion's Final Rising

The final Irathiro is not just the rising of Christ alone but the rising of His Body, the Bride, clothed with His light. Zion is not just a mountain; it is the perfected assembly, the mind of the redeemed aligned with the heart of Jerusalem.

The prophecy of Isaiah comes true:

> "Arise, shine; for thy light is come, and the glory of the LORD is risen upon thee." (Isaiah 60:1)

This is the rising of Irathiro in its purest form: the light of Christ in His people, a kingdom of shining stars who will reign forever with Him.

The East Gate becomes eternal. The throne is set. The Morning Star is never dimmed. And the nations walk in the light of Zion, for the Lamb is the lamp thereof.

Prophetic Key of Irathiro:
The story of the stars ends where it began — in the rising light of the East. What was shadowed in Eden, fought in Babel, promised to Abraham, dreamed by Joseph, prophesied by Balaam, corrupted by Lucifer, seen by Ezekiel, and warred in Daniel — is now fulfilled in Christ. The Bright Morning Star has returned, and His rising is eternal.

PART VII

AFRICA — IRATHIRO DESTINY

CHAPTER 19

Eden's Rivers and Africa's East Mandate

1 Edenic Geography — Africa as Eastward Prophetic Womb

The Word declares: "And the LORD God planted a garden eastward in Eden; and there he put the man whom he had formed." (Genesis 2:8). Eastward was not random; it was intentional. East is the gate of beginnings, the womb of first light.

When the rivers of Eden are described, one river encompasses the whole land of Cush (**Genesis 2:13**). Cush — the ancient heart of Africa — stands as the prophetic witness that Eden's waters nourished Africa directly. The rivers flowing from Eden were not only streams of water but streams of mandate. The eastward planting of Eden was mirrored in the eastward flow of its rivers, and Africa was one of the first wombs kissed by these waters.

Thus, Africa carries within her soil the echo of Eden. She is not peripheral — she is foundational. Her mandate is womb-like: to preserve the memory of first light, to be the keeper of the Irathiro prophecy, waiting for its resurrection.

2 Cush, Gihon, and the Cradle of Light

The river Gihon — named as encompassing the whole land of Cush — testifies that Eden's glory watered Africa. This is not accident but covenant geography. Cush becomes the cradle of Irathiro, the land where first light and first waters converged.

In prophetic language, rivers represent Spirit-flow. The Spirit moved in Eden, and those waters that touched Cush signify that the Spirit marked Africa with a covenant of life and destiny. Cush carried light, though history buried it under conquest, idolatry, and chains.

Africa's womb was attacked because it carried seed. The scattering at Babel tried to erase it. Egypt's oppression tried to cage it. Colonialism tried to silence it. But the cradle of light cannot be extinguished — the Gihon still speaks, calling Africa to arise in her east star mandate.

3 Africa's East Star Mandate

In Kikuyu prophetic tongue, *Irathiro* means east — the rising of the sun, the first break of light. Africa, positioned in the eastward womb of Eden's geography, carries a prophetic assignment: to rise as a constellation of redeemed stars in the last days.

The wise men who came from the East (**Matthew 2:2**) carried the testimony that the East would bear witness to Christ's birth. In the same way, Africa's east star mandate is to bear witness to Christ's return. From Ethiopia's eunuch (**Acts 8**), who carried the gospel back into Africa, to the prophecies of Cush stretching her hands unto God (*Psalm 68:31*), the scriptural pattern is clear: **Africa must rise as Irathiro in the last days.**

This mandate is both glory and warfare. Africa must resist counterfeit stars — ancestral idols, false prophets, and Babylonian systems and instead align her light with the Bright Morning Star. For the courtroom of heaven is reopening the case of Eden, and Africa is called as a star witness.

Prophetic Key of Irathiro:
Africa is not an afterthought in the story of God; she is Eden's witness. The Gihon's flow marks her as covenant ground, destined to rise as Irathiro. Africa's rising is not political first, but prophetic — a rising of holy stars aligned to Christ, bearing the light of the east to the ends of the earth.

CHAPTER 20

Kikuyu Prophecy of Irathiro

1 Kikuyu Language and Spiritual Codes of *Irathiro*

In Kikuyu prophetic tongue, Irathiro means East — the rising place of the sun, the beginning of light, the womb of morning. But in the deeper code of the Spirit, Irathiro is not merely direction; it is destiny.

- East is where Eden was planted (**Genesis 2:8**).
- East is where the glory of God enters His temple (**Ezekiel 43:2**).
- East is where wise men sought the star of Christ (**Matthew 2:2**).

Thus, when the Kikuyu tongue speaks *Irathiro*, it is unknowingly echoing the divine courtroom of Scripture — testifying that the **rising of the East** is the seal of God's prophetic order. The Kikuyu language itself is a vessel, carrying in sound and syllable the covenant code of the rising star.

Prophetic truth: languages are not accidents. They carry memory. The word *Irathiro* is itself a scroll, preserved in Kikuyu, waiting for the hour of unveiling.

2 East as Womb of Nations

The East is the **birthing ground** of nations. The Bible consistently ties eastward movement to beginnings:

- Eden eastward (**Genesis 2:8**) — womb of humanity.
- Abraham journeying eastward (**Genesis 12**) — womb of covenant.
- Israel encamped eastward before the tabernacle (**Numbers 2:3**) — womb of worship.
- Christ born under the star of the East (**Matthew 2:2**) — womb of salvation.

In the same rhythm, Africa, as touched by the Gihon river, is prophetically eastward — the womb of nations. She has birthed languages, peoples, and civilisations. Her pain in slavery and colonisation was the travail of a womb under attack, but her destiny is not barrenness — it is **fruitfulness in stars.**

The Kikuyu prophecy of Irathiro testifies that nations must look back to the East — to Africa — to see the rising of God's star in the last days.

3 Africa as Rising Holy Star in the Last Days

Psalm 68:31 declares: **"Princes shall come out of Egypt; Ethiopia (Cush) shall soon stretch out her hands unto God."** This is Irathiro language. Africa stretching her hands is the rising of the east star — the holy constellation appearing on the stage of the last days.

The Kikuyu people, standing at the gateway of East Africa beneath the shadow of Mount Kenya, hold a prophetic role as custodians of this revelation. Mount Kenya itself, capped in white snow, is a witness of Irathiro: a mountain of purity rising toward the heavens, reflecting the first light of every dawn. It is no coincidence that in Kikuyu tradition, prayers were often lifted facing the mountain, awaiting the God of Kirinyaga — the God of the mountain, who rises with the sun.

Now in Christ, that shadow is fulfilled: the true God of Zion rises as the Bright Morning Star, and Africa's eastward gaze becomes alignment with His eternal Irathiro. The Kikuyu prophecy becomes a trumpet, calling Africa to rise not in tribalism but in holy constellation — a company of stars aligned to the Lamb.

Africa's Irathiro destiny is not political dominion but **spiritual witness**. Her stars are not for astrology but for testimony. Her rising is not to exalt herself, but to declare to the nations: *The Bright Morning Star has risen, and His light shines from the East to the ends of the earth.*

Prophetic Key of Irathiro:
The Kikuyu word itself is a scroll. *Irathiro* is both language and prophecy, both geography and mandate. In the last days, Africa rises as Irathiro — a holy star constellation aligned with Christ. What was hidden in Eden's geography, whispered in Babel, fought in Egypt, and buried under oppression is now resurrected: the East is rising, and Africa is its witness.

CHAPTER 21

Separating Holy Stars from Wandering Stars

1 Jude 1:13 — **Wandering Stars Reserved for Darkness**

The apostle Jude warns: "Raging waves of the sea, foaming out their own shame; wandering stars, to whom is reserved the blackness of darkness for ever."

Here, stars represent destinies. Some shine faithfully in their appointed course, like the sun, moon, and constellations set in order on the fourth day (Genesis 1:16–18). Others rebel from alignment, drifting without orbit, becoming wandering stars.

Wandering stars are souls that abandon God's order, leaving their appointed habitation. They are compared to fallen angels (*Jude 1:6*), whose rebellion against divine placement made them outcasts of heaven's constellation.

These wandering stars are marked for judgment — not as celestial lights, but as eternal black holes of darkness.

Prophetic truth: not every rising star is holy. Some risings are counterfeit, birthed in rebellion, reserved for shadow.

2 Rising of True Sons as Holy Stars (*Romans 8*)

Paul declares in *Romans 8:19*: **"For the earnest expectation of the creature waiteth for the manifestation of the sons of God."** Creation groans for the holy stars to appear true sons who shine with the light of Christ, not the imitation of Lucifer.

These are not wandering stars but rooted stars: fixed in the constellation of Christ, aligned with the Bright Morning Star. They shine in order, in obedience, in covenant. Their rising is not self-glory but God's glory. They are lights in the world (*Philippians 2:15*), shining in a crooked generation.

Prophetic revelation: True sons are stars who have passed through death and resurrection, just as Christ the Morning Star rose through the grave. They are not independent luminaries but reflections of the One Light.

3 Judgment on Counterfeit Stars

The last days are courtroom days. Every star must be weighed. *Isaiah 34:4* prophesies: **"And all the host of heaven shall be dissolved, and the heavens shall be rolled together as a scroll: and all their host shall fall down, as the leaf falleth off from the vine."**

The dragon swept a third of the stars (*Revelation 12:4*), marking their rebellion. But judgment is clear: wandering stars cannot remain in orbit. They are cast down, bound, and silenced. The counterfeit constellations of sorcery, astrology, and false prophecy are dismantled, while the holy stars shine brighter unto eternal day (*Proverbs 4:18*).

The separation is not optional — it is divine decree. The courtroom of Irathiro ensures that only aligned stars remain, while the wandering ones fall into judgment.

Prophetic Key of Irathiro:
The East rising is not a mixed rising. Holy stars must be separated from wandering stars. True Irathiro is a constellation of redeemed sons, aligned to Christ the Bright Morning Star. Wandering stars, though they glitter for a moment, end in darkness. But holy stars, rooted in the covenant, rise forever in Zion's glory.

PART VIII

THE MANIFESTATION OF ZION

CHAPTER 22

Zion — The Mountain of Stars

1 Zion as Eastward Mountain of God

ll through Scripture, eastward mountains testify of divine meetings.

- Eden's garden was eastward (***Genesis 2:8***).

- Abraham saw Moriah, the mountain of sacrifice, eastward (***Genesis 22***).

- Ezekiel beheld the glory of God entering through the East Gate (***Ezekiel 43:2***).

- Christ ascended from the Mount of Olives, east of Jerusalem (***Acts 1:12***).

Zion is the culmination of all these eastward altars. It is not only a geographical mountain but the spiritual Irathiro, the eternal place where God sets His throne. **"For the LORD hath chosen Zion; he hath desired it for his habitation."** (***Psalm 132:13***).

Thus Zion becomes the **mountain of stars**, the high place where redeemed sons, shining as constellations, gather in worship. The mountain is clothed in light, and its summit glows with the rising of the Bright Morning Star.

And here is a prophetic witness from the earth: **Mount Kenya** rises on the eastern backbone of Africa. Though it sits nearly on the equator, its massif leans eastward of the Great Rift Valley. Its glaciers and slopes give birth to rivers that flow like living parables. From its eastern face descends the mighty **Tana River**, coursing eastward toward the Indian Ocean — the sunrise gate. From its northern slopes flows the **Ewaso Nyiro River**, turning northward into the wilderness, watering dry lands. Together they form a witness: waters proceeding from an **eastward mountain**, flowing outward to bless the nations.

In prophetic language, Mount Kenya is an *eastward mountain*: a natural mirror of Zion, a high place where earth itself seems to incline toward the rising light. As Irathiro means *East Rising*, this geography testifies that God planted a witness in the land to echo the heavenly Zion.

2 Streams of Mount Kenya as Prophetic Echo of Zion's River

The psalmist declared: *"There is a river, the streams whereof shall make glad the city of God, the holy place of the tabernacles of the most High."* (**Psalm 46:4**).

In Revelation, John saw the fulfillment: *"And he shewed me a pure river of water of life, clear as crystal, proceeding out of the throne of God and of the Lamb."* (**Revelation 22:1**). Out of Zion flows the eternal river, whose streams bring healing and gladness to all creation.

Now consider Mount Kenya's witness:

- The **Tana River**, descending eastward, mirrors the river of God flowing toward the sunrise — the place of resurrection, hope, and the nations' awakening.

- The **Ewaso Nyiro**, flowing northward into the wilderness, mirrors the stream that reaches barren lands, turning deserts into gardens — a sign of restoration for the dry and desolate.

- Other streams, breaking from the mountain in every direction, mirror the prophecy of *Ezekiel 47*, where the waters from the temple spread outward, deepening until they become a river that no man can pass over.

Thus, Africa's highest sacred massif becomes a natural icon of Zion's mystery: **a mountain releasing streams, making the nations glad.** Just as the psalmist saw rivers gladdening the city of God, so the rivers of Mount Kenya proclaim that Africa is not a wilderness forgotten but a womb of rivers, a prophetic Irathiro aligned with Zion's throne.

3 God's Throne Shining as Eternal Constellation

John in Revelation beholds a throne encircled by stars, a rainbow like an emerald, and a sea of glass mingled with fiery streams (*Revelation 4:3–6*). The throne is not solitary; it is encircled by stars, elders, angels, and living creatures, each reflecting the radiance of the King.

Daniel also foresaw this: **"A fiery stream issued and came forth from before him: thousand thousands ministered unto him, and ten thousand times ten thousand stood before him."** (*Daniel 7:10*). These are not wandering lights but ordered stars in His courtroom constellation.

Zion's throne is therefore not a static or chair but a cosmos, a constellation of order, radiance, and harmony, **flowing**: radiance streams outward, order radiates, rivers proceed. The throne shines, and every aligned star takes its appointed place, forming the eternal government of God; it is a constellation, a cosmos of light and life. In heaven, this fiery stream is Spirit; on earth, the rivers of Mount Kenya give us a prophetic shadow of that eternal stream.

4 Sabbath Rest as the Seal of Rising Stars

At the heart of Zion's constellation lies the mystery of rest. For no star shines by striving, stars shine by placement. And the placement of the redeemed is sealed in **Sabbath rest**.

> *"This is the rest wherewith ye may cause the weary to rest; and this is the refreshing." (Isaiah 28:12).*

The Sabbath is not only a day but a seal, the signature of the Spirit that distinguishes holy stars from wandering ones.

In Zion, the river flows because the throne rests, and every rising star rests in God. The streams proceed not from labour, but from alignment. So too, from Mount Kenya's resting glaciers flow rivers without toil, bearing testimony that when God sets a mountain in His covenant, waters must flow. The war of constellations is over. The dragon is cast down, Babylon's lights extinguished, wandering stars judged. Only the constellation of the Lamb remains, shining in Sabbath glory.

Thus, Zion's rising is not toil but rest, not ambition but alignment. To be a star in Zion is to be at peace in God's eternal light, sealed by His Sabbath covenant.

Prophetic Key of Irathiro:
Zion is the final eastward mountain, the eternal constellation where holy stars shine forever. God's throne is the centre, His glory the light, His Sabbath the seal.

On earth, Mount Kenya stands as a prophetic echo: an eastward massif leaning toward the sunrise, releasing rivers eastward like streams of glory toward sunrise and wilderness alike. Its rivers mirror *Psalm 46:4* and *Revelation 22:1* — the streams that gladden the city of God.

In heaven, Zion's summit glows with the Bright Morning Star. In both realms, **Irathiro is fulfilled**: the East rising becomes eternal light, and the stars of the covenant rest in unending day.

Thus, Africa bears witness to heaven: Zion's river has an earthly shadow, and Irathiro's east star mandate is confirmed in stone, in water, in mountain. The throne above and the rivers below sing one testimony — **the rising of eternal light, and the sealing of the stars in Sabbath rest.**

CHAPTER 23

The Bride Shining as Stars

1 Church as Clothed with Sun, Crowned with Stars (*Revelation 12:1*)

John beholds a great wonder in heaven:

"A woman clothed with the sun, and the moon under her feet, and upon her head a crown of twelve stars." (Revelation 12:1).

This woman is the **Church as the Bride**, not yet in her final marriage supper, but already radiant in her testimony. She is clothed with the **sun of righteousness** — the light of Christ Himself. She stands above the moon — not ruled by cycles, shadows, or borrowed lights, but established in eternal day.

And her head bears a **crown of twelve stars** — the constellation of Israel fulfilled in the Church, the full government of God reflected in redeemed humanity. This is the Bride of Irathiro, radiant with the first light and the last light, clothed in the eternal sun and crowned with the stars of covenant.

2 Holy Stars as the Bride's Crown

Every redeemed son and daughter shines in this constellation. As it is written in Daniel, *"They that turn many to righteousness shall shine as the stars for ever and ever."* (**Daniel 12:3**). These stars are not wandering lights but aligned ones, set as a crown of testimony on the Bride's head.

The **twelve-star crown** is not merely a number but a fullness:

- Twelve tribes of Israel.
- Twelve apostles of the Lamb.
- Twelve foundations of the New Jerusalem.
- Twelve gates by which nations enter in.

Together, these become the Bride's diadem, the constellation of God's government resting upon her. What Lucifer once sought in pride, a throne among the stars (**Isaiah 14:13**) — the Bride now receives in humility, as a gift from the Bridegroom.

3 Final Manifestation of Irathiro Glory

In this vision, **Irathiro reaches its climax**. The eastward rising of holy stars finds its consummation in the Bride, who shines not with borrowed light but with her Husband's glory. The woman of *Revelation 12* is the **Church transfigured**: crowned with stars, prepared to give birth to a kingdom, radiant as Zion's companion.

The dragon still rages, sweeping his tail against the stars (***Revelation 12:4***). Yet he cannot extinguish the crown, for these stars are sealed in Sabbath rest, aligned in the Lamb's constellation. The Bride stands, luminous, crowned, and immovable.

Thus, the **final manifestation of Irathiro** is not a star in isolation but a Bride in union, clothed with the Sun of Righteousness, standing above the moon of temporal powers, and crowned with the eternal constellation of holy stars.

Prophetic Key of Irathiro:
The Bride is the living constellation of God. Her star-crown testifies that Irathiro glory is not scattered but gathered, not wandering but aligned, not temporal but eternal. When the Bride shines, the whole creation beholds the East fulfilled: **the rising of holy stars in the crown of eternal light.**

CHAPTER 24

The Eternal Star of the Lamb

1 Christ as Alpha-East and Omega-Light

When Jesus declares, "I am Alpha and Omega, the beginning and the end, the first and the last" (Revelation 22:13), He identifies Himself as the Alpha-East; the first light of creation and the Omega-Light — the final illumination of eternity.

In Him, Irathiro is both origin and destiny. The rising of the East that began in Eden, that journeyed through Abraham, Jacob, Joseph, the prophets, and the Bride, is fulfilled in the Lamb who is both **the Bright and Morning Star** (*Revelation 22:16*) and the **eternal Sun** whose light never sets (*Revelation 21:23*).

The Lamb is not one star among many — He is the star that births all others, the centre of the constellation, the eternal Irathiro.

2 They that Turn Many to Righteousness Shall Shine Forever (*Daniel 12:3*)

The testimony of Daniel is now unveiled in fullness: *"They that be wise shall shine as the brightness of the firmament; and they that turn many to righteousness as the stars for ever and ever."*

The redeemed are not fading sparks but eternal flames. Their light is not self-generated but borrowed from the Lamb, whose radiance they reflect. To turn many to righteousness is to join the Lamb in His eastward work — to gather stars into His constellation, to align wandering lights into the orbit of Zion's throne.

Thus the eternal destiny of holy stars is not survival but **government**: to shine forever as witnesses of the Lamb's reign.

3 Final Decree: The Stars from Irathiro Shall Reign in Zion

The story closes where it began: in Irathiro. What was once the rising place of the sun becomes now the **eternal dwelling of stars**. From Eden's eastward garden to Mount Zion's eternal throne, the narrative has been one long sunrise, the dawn of God's covenant, now risen into eternal day.

The decree of heaven resounds: **The Stars from Irathiro shall reign in Zion.**

- Not wandering but seated.
- Not fading but everlasting.
- Not scattered but gathered.
- Not striving but resting.

The Lamb is the Eternal Star, and in Him the stars of the covenant shine forever. Zion's mountain glows with constellations of redeemed sons, the Bride crowned with eternal light, and the nations walking in the radiance of the New Jerusalem.

Prophetic Key of Irathiro:

Christ the Lamb is the Alpha-East and the Omega-Light. In Him, Irathiro is completed: the stars rise, align, and reign forever in Zion. The decree is final — **the holy stars from the East shall never set.**

BONUS PART

THE FINAL WITNESS OF IRATHIRO

CHAPTER 25

Pentecost — Stars Poured Out, the Spirit's Irathiro

1 The Outpouring of the Spirit as the Multiplication of Stars (*Acts 2*)

When the Spirit descended at Pentecost, it was not just tongues of fire upon a few, but the birthing of a new constellation. For the promise of Christ "Ye shall receive power, after that the Holy Ghost is come upon you" (Acts 1:8) was the promise of a sky no longer dark, but ablaze with lights.

Acts 2 records that *"there appeared unto them cloven tongues like as of fire, and it sat upon each of them."* Each believer became a star ignited. No longer was light reserved for the prophets or kings of old the Spirit democratised fire. A whole assembly became a galaxy, the upper room a sky.

Pentecost was therefore Irathiro fulfilled in Spirit. Just as the sun rises in the east and scatters its rays across the heavens, so the Spirit rose as the Morning Star of the Church, scattering lights across nations. What was once one star, Christ the Bright and Morning Star now multiplied into many through His Spirit, shining across earth's firmament.

2 The Church Becomes a Sky Filled with Lights

Paul declared, *"Ye shine as lights in the world; holding forth the word of life"* (**Philippians 2:15–16**). This is Pentecostal identity: the Church not as a single lamp, but as constellations.

In **Revelation 1**, John beheld Christ walking among lampstands, holding seven stars in His right hand. These were the angels and witnesses of the churches, set as lights in the darkness of empire. Pentecost birthed not one lampstand but seven, not one star but multitudes each burning with the oil of the Spirit.

Thus the Body of Christ is not a scattered crowd but an ordered cosmos, a constellation aligned around the Lamb. Every witness, every prayer, every tongue of fire, adds to the sky. Pentecost is heaven's night-sky filled with holy stars, a foretaste of Zion's eternal constellation.

3 Kenya and Africa's Eastward Destiny as the Pentecostal Womb

Here Irathiro speaks with final clarity. For Pentecost began in Jerusalem, but its light was never meant to remain there. It was eastward in birth, westward in spread, and now eastward again in consummation.

Africa, and Kenya in particular carries this eastward womb. For Kenya is the only nation named after a mountain, and that mountain leans eastward. Its rivers flow like living streams to the nations, echoing the river from Zion's throne (**Psalm 46:4, Revelation 22:1–2**).

Pentecost's prophecy is this: the same fire that fell in Jerusalem will have its last-day echo in Africa. Kenya, as Irathiro, becomes the womb of the final revival, where the Spirit is poured again in multiplied measure. From the slopes of Mount Kenya to the ends of the earth, a sky of stars shall rise; a multitude of burning witnesses, filling the global firmament before the end comes.

As Joel foresaw: *"And it shall come to pass afterward, that I will pour out my spirit upon all flesh; and your sons and your daughters shall prophesy"* (**Joel 2:28**). Kenya's destiny is to be the east gate through which this prophecy culminates; a last Pentecost, an Irathiro Pentecost, a rising of stars poured out without measure.

Prophetic Key of Irathiro:
Pentecost was the dawn of stars; the last Pentecost is their noonday shining. Kenya, as the mountain of Irathiro, stands as the womb of this final constellation. The Spirit poured once in Jerusalem shall be poured last in Africa, and the Church shall shine as an innumerable sky, the stars of Irathiro filling the earth with glory.

CHAPTER 26

The Crown of Twelve Stars — The Woman in Travail (Revelation 12)

1 The Bride Clothed with the Sun, Crowned with Twelve Stars

John beholds a mystery in heaven: "a woman clothed with the sun, and the moon under her feet, and upon her head a crown of twelve stars" (Revelation 12:1). This woman is not a mere symbol; she is the Bride, the Church, the Zion woman.

To be *clothed with the sun* is to wear Christ Himself, the righteousness of the Morning Star who rose in glory. To have *the moon under her feet* is to walk in dominion over reflected, lesser lights — the systems of shadow and borrowed power. And upon her head is the crown: twelve stars, the complete constellation of Israel fulfilled in the Church, the unity of tribes and apostles, the government of God as a diadem of light.

Here, the Irathiro mystery reaches fullness. From Abraham's promise of stars, to Joseph's dream of stars, to Daniel's prophecy of shining stars, the Bride now bears the entire constellation as a crown. She is the mountain of stars embodied, the Irathiro woman who rises in the courtroom of heaven, clothed in glory.

2 Travail Against the Dragon Beneath the Courtroom of Heaven

But the vision does not end in triumph alone. *"And she being with child cried, travailing in birth, and pained to be delivered"* (**Revelation 12:2**). The crown is not without the cross; the light is not without the labour.

The dragon — red, vast, seven-headed stands beneath her. With his tail, he seeks to drag a third of the stars from heaven (**Revelation 12:4**). Here is cosmic warfare: the serpent who first deceived Eve now confronts the Woman of Irathiro, the Bride who is Eve redeemed, Israel fulfilled, the Church transfigured.

The travail is both spiritual and global: the birth of the sons of God, the manifestation of the man-child destined *"to rule all nations with a rod of iron"* (**Revelation 12:5**). The courtroom of heaven hears the cry, and angels rise to contend with the dragon. Michael leads the holy stars in battle, and the woman's labour becomes the threshold of judgment.

3 The Warfare of Irathiro: The Rising Woman versus the Fallen Serpent

This is the final clash: Irathiro rising against the serpent's fall. The woman is eastward, crowned with the sunrise, clothed with the light of Christ, surrounded by the testimony of twelve stars. The dragon is westward, falling into darkness, consumed with rage because his time is short.

The war of constellations reaches its climax. The true crown; twelve holy stars is set upon the Bride. The false constellation, the dragon's sweep of fallen stars collapses into judgment.

Irathiro here becomes both womb and weapon. The Bride's travail is not in vain; the man-child is born, caught up to God and His throne. The dragon is cast down, and the accuser's voice silenced in the courtroom of heaven. The warfare is sealed by testimony: *"They overcame him by the blood of the Lamb, and by the word of their testimony"* (**Revelation 12:11**).

Thus, the stars of Irathiro do not merely shine they war. Their crown is also their sword, their light also their decree. And in their travail, the destiny of nations is determined.

Prophetic Key of Irathiro:
The Bride crowned with twelve stars is the final Irathiro constellation, the complete order of God, shining in the courtroom of heaven. Her travail is the birth of sons, her crown is the testimony of tribes and apostles, and her warfare is the overthrow of the dragon. In her rising, the serpent falls, and Irathiro's glory is revealed as both crown and victory.

CHAPTER 27

The Beast and the False Constellations

1 *Revelation 13* — Beast Systems Claiming Star-Authority

When the dragon is cast down, he does not rest. His fury gives birth to beast systems. John records:

> "And I stood upon the sand of the sea, and saw a beast rise up out of the sea, having seven heads and ten horns, and upon his horns ten crowns…" (Revelation 13:1).

The dragon lost the stars of heaven, so he creates his counterfeit constellations on earth. These horns and crowns mimic the glory of Zion's stars but are rooted in rebellion. This is the beast — political empires, economic systems, and religious powers fused into one global dominion.

Notice the progression: the dragon seeks worship but has no throne of his own, so he empowers the beast. The beast becomes his constellation, his imitation of Irathiro. Where God crowns the Bride with twelve stars, the dragon crowns the beast with ten horns. The counterfeit constellation rises, but it cannot replace Zion's crown.

2 Counterfeit Signs and Constellations That Try to Eclipse Zion's Crown

John testifies that the beast performs signs and wonders: *"And he doeth great wonders, so that he maketh fire come down from heaven on the earth in the sight of men"* (**Revelation 13:13**). These are **false stars** — counterfeit lights meant to deceive the nations.

Like Nimrod building Babel, the beast system constructs false constellations of power:

- **Political stars** — kings and rulers aligned in rebellion.
- **Economic stars** — merchants and markets bound by mammon.
- **Religious stars** — prophets of lies, false teachers, and counterfeit altars.

Together they form Babylon's sky; a constellation of confusion, seduction, and oppression. These stars are not fixed in Zion's order but wander in rebellion, luring nations into darkness.

The beast marks men with his counterfeit seal, attempting to eclipse the **Sabbath seal of Zion**. The mark of the beast is a false star upon the hand and forehead, a counterfeit of the true alignment of the mind and works in God's rest.

Judgment Decreed Against False Star Systems

But heaven has already issued its verdict. The beast rises only for a season, for his constellation has no root in the eternal Irathiro. John hears another voice from heaven: *"Babylon the great is fallen, is fallen, and is become the habitation of devils"* (**Revelation 18:2**).

The courtroom of Zion decrees judgment against every false star system:

- **Political stars will fall** — kings of the earth hiding from the face of the Lamb (***Revelation 6:15***).

- **Economic stars will collapse** — merchants weeping as Babylon burns (***Revelation 18:11***).

- **Religious stars will be judged** — false prophets cast into the lake of fire with the beast (***Revelation 19:20***).

The dragon's counterfeit constellation will be extinguished. Only the Lamb's stars, sealed in Sabbath rest, will shine forever.

Prophetic Key of Irathiro:
The beast is the dragon's counterfeit constellation, a false crown of horns and signs. But Irathiro's decree is final: Zion's twelve stars will outshine Babylon's false heavens. The Bride's crown cannot be eclipsed. The courtroom has spoken. Every wandering star will fall, and only the constellation of the Lamb shall remain.

CHAPTER 28

Babylon the Queen of Stars

1 *Revelation 17* — The Harlot Clothed in False Glory

John beholds the woman:

"arrayed in purple and scarlet, and decked with gold and precious stones and pearls, having a golden cup in her hand full of abominations and filthiness of her fornication" (Revelation 17:4).

Here is Babylon personified; the great harlot, seated upon many waters, riding the beast of false constellations. She is clothed not in the radiance of Christ but in imitation, purple without priesthood, scarlet without sacrifice, jewels without true fire.

Her cup gleams with golden brilliance, but it is filled with poison. Nations drink, kings fornicate, and merchants enrich themselves under her shining. She presents herself as a star-queen, but she is no bride; she is a counterfeit crowned in corruption.

2 Babylon Sitting as Counterfeit "Star-Queen"

Babylon positions herself as a rival constellation, a queen who pretends to sit in the place of Irathiro: *"I sit a queen, and am no widow, and shall see no sorrow"* (**Revelation 18:7**).

She gathers nations under her false light. Her constellations are:

- **Cultural stars** — philosophies, arts, and sciences stripped of God's glory.
- **Political stars** — kings aligned with her harlotry.
- **Economic stars** — merchants made rich through her luxury.
- **Religious stars** — priests and prophets corrupted by her wine.

She crowns herself with borrowed jewels, imitating the twelve-star crown of the Bride. But her stars are not living lights; they are dead stones, cut and fashioned by man, lacking the Spirit's fire.

Babylon is therefore the counterfeit "queen of stars," sitting on the beast, presiding over the dragon's rebellion. She is the fallen Irathiro, the east turned west, the light turned into darkness.

3 The Fall of Babylon's Constellations Before Zion's True Bride

But heaven proclaims a decree:

> *"Babylon the great is fallen, is fallen, and is become the habitation of devils"* (Revelation 18:2).

The courtroom verdict is final:

- Her **cultural stars** are extinguished — music silenced, craftsmen vanished (**Revelation 18:22**).
- Her **economic stars** collapse — merchants weep as their markets burn (**Revelation 18:11**).

- Her **political stars** turn against her — the beast she rides devours her flesh (***Revelation 17:16***).

- Her **religious stars** are judged — the false prophets fall into the lake of fire.

The harlot is dethroned, the false crown stripped. Her stars fade into eternal darkness, while Zion's Bride rises clothed in white linen, crowned with true constellations of light.

The marriage of the Lamb eclipses the harlot's feast. The wine of Babylon's fornication gives way to the wine of the kingdom. The queen of false stars falls, and the Bride of true stars reigns.

Prophetic Key of Irathiro:
Babylon is the counterfeit queen of stars, shining with stolen jewels, riding the beast's constellation. But her fall is decreed. Zion's Bride, crowned with twelve living stars, rises as the true Queen, clothed in the sun and sealed in Sabbath rest. The harlot descends into darkness, but the Bride ascends into everlasting light.

CHAPTER 29

Egypt, Exodus, and the War of Stars

1 Pharaoh's Magicians as Counterfeit Stars

When Moses entered Pharaoh's court, the confrontation was more than political; it was cosmic. Pharaoh's magicians stretched forth their rods, mimicking the signs of heaven. They were Egypt's "constellations" priests of Ra, scribes of Thoth, keepers of the stars.

Their rods became serpents; their waters turned to blood. They claimed the authority of light, the wisdom of the Nile, the brilliance of Egypt's constellations. But these were counterfeit stars, false illuminations birthed from the dragon's breath.

The plagues of Egypt were not random acts of judgment. Each plague struck down one of Egypt's false constellations:

- The Nile (Hapi) darkened — the river-star eclipsed.

- Frogs (Heqet) filled the land — the fertility-star disgraced.

- Darkness swallowed Ra — the sun-god himself blotted out.

Thus, Egypt's constellations collapsed, their counterfeit stars dimmed before the light of Yahweh.

2 Moses as a True East Star Leading Israel Out

In the eastward dawn, Moses rose as a true star. Not clothed in Egyptian jewels, but in the fire of Sinai's promise. He stretched forth the rod of God, and the heavens bore witness that the Red Sea parted, Israel passed, Egypt drowned.

Moses is Irathiro, a witness from Africa's soil, raised as a deliverer, leading God's people eastward toward covenant rest. His face shone with glory, like a star reflecting the sun. He was not a star for himself, but a pointer to the Greater Star even Christ Himself, the Morning Star.

As Balaam later prophesied: *"There shall come a Star out of Jacob, and a Sceptre shall rise out of Israel"* (**Numbers 24:17**). Moses was a shadow, Christ the substance.

3 Africa as the Battleground of Holy and False Constellations

Egypt reveals Africa's hidden role in prophecy: it is the soil where true and false stars contend.

- **False stars**: Pharaoh, magicians, idols, pyramids aligned with counterfeit heavens.
- **True star**: Moses, burning bush, rod of God, Passover Lamb pointing to Christ.

Africa has always been this arena.

- Joseph rose as a star in Egypt, saving nations.
- Israel was birthed in Egypt, nourished before exodus.
- Christ Himself fled into Egypt as a child, protected until the appointed time.

Thus, Africa is not marginal but central, the ground where

constellations clash. Egypt's counterfeit heavens were shattered by Yahweh's signs. And in the last days, Africa again rises as Irathiro, the witness of the true Star.

Prophetic Key of Irathiro

Egypt was the first Babylon, the mother of false constellations. But it was also the womb where deliverance arose. Africa's soil carries this duality, both counterfeit crowns and covenant births.

In the last days, Africa becomes Irathiro, the eastward witness. Kenya, crowned by the mountain that bears God's name, emerges as the last prophetic stage where the Bride rises clothed with the true stars.

The war of stars that began in Egypt ends in Zion, and Africa is the battlefield where the dragon falls, and the Bride ascends.

CHAPTER 30

Kenya — The Mountain of Irathiro

1 Kenya as the Only Nation Named After a Mountain

Among the nations, Kenya stands uniquely. Nations are named after kings, tribes, or lands, but Kenya alone bears the name of a mountain. This is no accident. For Scripture declares: "Out of Zion, the perfection of beauty, God hath shined" (Psalm 50:2).

Mountains are God's chosen thrones on earth: Sinai, where the Law was given, Zion where His presence rests, Carmel where Elijah confronted Baal. In this same pattern, Mount Kenya becomes a prophetic altar, a throne-witness of God's covenant.

To be named after a mountain is to be marked as a nation of witness, a prophetic altar before the nations. Kenya carries in its very name the destiny of Irathiro, the rising of the East.

2 Mount Kenya as a Prophetic Eastward Altar

From Mount Kenya flow rivers like the streams of Zion:

- **The Tana River** — flowing eastward, echoing Eden's river that parted and watered the earth (*Genesis 2:10*).

- **The Ewaso Nyiro** — flowing north, mirroring Ezekiel's river that healed the desert and gave life to the nations (***Ezekiel 47***).

- **The streams of Irathiro** — fulfilling ***Psalm 46:4***: *"There is a river, the streams whereof shall make glad the city of God."*

Thus, Mount Kenya is not just a physical peak but a prophetic fountain. Its snowcap, white with witness, points to Christ's glory. Its rivers declare the outflow of the Spirit. Its eastward position marks it as a sunrise altar, the morning star of Africa.

3 Kenya as the Last Typology of Israel

As Israel was chosen to bear God's covenant to the nations, so Kenya rises as a last-day typology, an Irathiro-Israel.

- Israel was a nation of covenant. Kenya is rising as a nation of prayer.

- Israel was crowned with Jerusalem. Kenya is crowned with Mount Kenya.

- Israel bore witness to the Messiah's first coming. Kenya bears witness to His last-day outpouring.

Kenya is not replacing Israel but mirroring her role as a prophetic echo, a typology. For the last shall be first, and God's eastward witness shall confirm His covenant to the ends of the earth.

4 The Womb of Last-Day Revival

Africa has long carried a prophetic seed. Egypt nourished Israel. Ethiopia carried the Ark in her witness. Now Kenya, as the mountain-nation, becomes the womb of the last-day revival.

From her soil, prayers rise like incense. From her rivers, the Spirit flows to nations. From her altar, a global fire shall break forth.

The Bride clothed with the sun shall find her eastward rising in Kenya — Irathiro. This is not merely revival but the final outpouring, the Pentecost of nations, the Sabbath glory covering the earth as waters cover the sea.

Prophetic Seal of Irathiro

Kenya is Irathiro, the east star, the mountain witness, the nation clothed with Sabbath light. As Israel carried the first covenant, Kenya carries the final witness of the Spirit.

The dragon rages, Babylon falls, Egypt trembles, but from Kenya the Irathiro flame ascends. And the stars of Africa, multiplied in Pentecost, shall fill the heavens with glory until the Bride is crowned, and the Lamb is enthroned.

CHAPTER 31

Zion's Constellation of Twelve Stars

1 The Bride Crowned with Twelve (*Revelation 12:1*)

"And there appeared a great wonder in heaven; a woman clothed with the sun, and the moon under her feet, and upon her head a crown of twelve stars."

This woman is not an earthly queen but the heavenly Bride, the Church in her fullness. She is clothed with the sun of righteousness (Malachi 4:2), walking in the light of Christ Himself. She has the moon, time and seasons under her feet, no longer bound by cycles of shadow. And she wears upon her head a crown of twelve stars, the complete constellation of God's covenant order.

The Irathiro rising culminates here: the east star that began as Abraham's faith, passed through Israel's tribes, shone in Christ, multiplied in Pentecost, and is now gathered into one crown upon the Bride.

2 The Twelve Tribes, Twelve Apostles, Twelve Gates, Twelve

Foundations

The constellation of twelve is not arbitrary; it is God's eternal number of government, His signature of completeness.

- **Twelve Tribes** — Israel's covenant sons, foundations of identity.

- **Twelve Apostles** — the New Covenant witnesses, pillars of testimony.

- **Twelve Gates** — access into the eternal city, each gate a tribe, each entry a witness.

- **Twelve Foundations** — the apostolic strata of Zion's temple, each layer embedded with a name and a stone (***Revelation 21:19-20***).

Together they form not just a number but a constellation, the ordered stars of Zion, a heavenly government, a bridal crown.

Thus, when ***Revelation 12*** shows the woman crowned with twelve stars, it is declaring that God's order is complete, His Bride fully adorned, His government fully established in heaven and on earth.

3 Zion as the Complete Constellation of Irathiro Order

Zion is more than a mountain; it is the city, the temple, the constellation. The stars aligned in Zion are not wandering but ordered. Each tribe, each apostle, each stone, each gate shines in harmony.

The Irathiro mystery is perfected here:

- The eastward rising (Genesis 2:8) finds its eternal throne (***Psalm 132:13***).

- The stars of Abraham's seed (Genesis 15:5) gather into the Lamb's constellation (***Revelation 21:23***).

- The crown of twelve completes the Bride's travail and triumph over the dragon (**Revelation 12:4–6**).

Thus, Zion becomes the universe's final constellation — the true Irathiro. Not Babylon's counterfeit jewels, not Egypt's magicians, not the beast's false signs, but the radiant Bride crowned with the stars of God's order.

4 The Bride's Final Glory

The Bride crowned with twelve stars, is not a hidden remnant but a global witness. She shines with Irathiro light, eastward glory that fills the world. The dragon may rage beneath, but he cannot eclipse the constellation above.

For the testimony is sealed:

> *"They that be wise shall shine as the brightness of the firmament; and they that turn many to righteousness as the stars forever and ever." (Daniel 12:3).*

The Bride is this fulfilment, the constellation of Zion, the holy stars sealed in Sabbath rest, shining eternally in the Lamb's light.

Prophetic Seal of Irathiro:
The crown of twelve is the seal of completion. The Bride is no longer in travail but in triumph. Zion shines as the final constellation, the eternal Irathiro order, where the Lamb and His Bride reign forever.

CHAPTER 32

The Marriage Supper of the Lamb — The Gathering of Stars

1 The Wedding Feast as Constellation-Gathering (*Revelation 19*)

> *"Let us be glad and rejoice, and give honour to him: for the marriage of the Lamb is come, and his wife hath made herself ready." (Revelation 19:7)*

The vision shifts from warfare to wedding. From the travail of the woman to the triumph of the Bride. From stars struggling against the dragon to stars gathered into the feast of eternity.

This is not a banquet of food but of glory, the marriage supper of the Lamb is the great constellation-gathering, where every redeemed star takes its seat, aligned in order, clothed in fine linen "clean and white: for the fine linen is the righteousness of saints." (***Revelation 19:8***).

Here, the Bride becomes more than adorned; she becomes united. She is no longer waiting eastward for the Morning Star; she is one with Him.

2 The Bride Enters Eternal Union with the Bright Morning Star

Christ declared,

> *"I am the root and the offspring of David, and the bright and morning star."* (Revelation 22:16).

At the marriage supper, this declaration becomes an eternal union. The Bride, who was crowned with twelve stars is now joined to the Morning Star Himself. The constellation is completed, not as a separate crown, but as one radiance with the Lamb.

- The **stars of Abraham's promise** (*Genesis 15:5*).
- The **crown of twelve** (*Revelation 12:1*).
- The **constellation of Zion** (*Revelation 21:23*).

All converge in one light: the Bride and the Lamb shining together as one eternal star, the Irathiro fulfilled forever.

3 The Stars of Irathiro Find Eternal Rest in Zion's Glory

Psalm 132:13–14 declares:

> *"For the LORD hath chosen Zion; he hath desired it for his habitation. This is my rest for ever: here will I dwell; for I have desired it."*

The marriage supper seals this rest. The war of stars is over. The dragon is cast down. Babylon has fallen. The beast is judged. And the Bride enters Sabbath without end, eternal Irathiro, eternal eastward glory.

The stars do not wander anymore; they are set in the Lamb's heavens. Their shining is no longer contested but consummated. Their crown is no longer for travail but for triumph. Their glory is not borrowed but eternal.

Thus, the marriage supper is not the end of history but the beginning of eternity, the dawning of unending Sabbath light, where Bride and Bridegroom shine as one constellation in Zion forever.

Prophetic Seal of Irathiro:
The Marriage Supper is the gathering of stars. The Bride and the Lamb are wed in eternal Sabbath, the stars of Irathiro resting forever in Zion's glory. The eastward rising has reached its full day, and there is no more night.

PRAYER

for Nationalisation into the Kingdom of Heaven

Scriptural Foundation:
- John 3:3 – "Jesus answered and said to him, 'Most assuredly, I say to you, unless one is born again, he cannot see the kingdom of God.'"

- Philippians 3:20 – "For our citizenship is in heaven, from which we also eagerly wait for the Savior, the Lord Jesus Christ."

- Ephesians 2:19 – "Now therefore you are no longer strangers and foreigners, but fellow citizens with the saints and members of the household of God."

- Colossians 1:13 – "He has delivered us from the power of darkness and conveyed us into the kingdom of the Son of His love."

- Romans 10:9 – "That if you confess with your mouth the Lord Jesus and believe in your heart that God has raised Him from the dead, you will be saved."

Righteous Judge of Heaven and Earth,

I come before Your throne, the **throne of Grace** in **the Court of Heaven**, in the name of Jesus Christ, my Lord and Saviour. I stand by the power of His precious blood, which has **redeemed me** and **bought my salvation**. I come humbly and boldly, desiring to be **nationalised into the Kingdom of Heaven**—to become a **true citizen of Your heavenly realm**.

Father, Your Word declares in **John 3:3** that **unless one is born again**, they cannot see the Kingdom of God. Today, **I renounce any citizenship** I once held in this world and any **ties to the powers of darkness**. I acknowledge that I have been **transferred from the kingdom of darkness into the Kingdom of the Son** of Your love (*Colossians 1:13*). I declare that I am no longer a stranger or foreigner, but a **fellow citizen with the saints** and a member of the household of God (*Ephesians 2:19*).

Lord Jesus, I believe with all my heart that You are the **Son of the living God**, that You died for my sins and rose again to grant me eternal life (**Romans 10:9**). I now receive You as my **personal Savior**, **my Redeemer**, **the only Way**, **the Truth**, and **the Life**. You are the **Door to the Father's heart** and the only **path to salvation**. I do not want to **perish** with the world, but to **live eternally with You**.

At this moment, I [Your Full Name] solemnly, sincerely, and truthfully affirm my love, my seriousness, and my desire to follow You and serve You in **holiness and righteousness**. I pledge my full allegiance to You, O King of kings and Lord of lords. I give my loyalty to the third Heaven and honour its **rights and freedoms**. I desire to settle with You, **Lord Jesus**. I repent of the way I have **lived my life and of all my sins**. Take over **my heart and my destiny**. Save me, cleanse me, and change me.

I beseech that You **seal my heavenly citizenship today**. Let the record of **my new identity** be **registered in the Court of Heaven**. Write my name in the **Lamb's Book of Life**, and erase it from the **book of death and judgment**. Let every **legal claim the enemy** has over my past be **cancelled** and **rendered powerless by the blood of Jesus**.

Lord, I am ready to walk the path of **righteousness and holiness**. I cast all **my cares and all of myself upon You**, for You care for me and loved me and laid Your life as the Lamb slain from **the foundation of the world**. Let Your **will be done** in my life as it is in Heaven.

By Your blood, I now receive eternal life. I proclaim that I am a **new creature**. By the word of Your testimony, I am made free indeed. **Fill me and baptize me** with the **Holy Ghost and fire**. Thank You, Lord Jesus, for giving me the right and the power to become a child of God, born **not of flesh but of the Spirit**, according to **the new covenant sealed in Your blood**.

I believe **You died** for me, and on the **third day**, You rose again. You are now seated at the right hand of the **Father in glory**, and I receive You as the Lord of my life. Through You, I have **received grace, peace, forgiveness, and eternal inheritance**. I stand holy, blameless, and without fault before the **Court of Heaven** because of the **righteousness imputed to me through Your sacrifice**.

Now, I **declare that the power of sin, death, and Satan—including the grave—**has been **broken over my life**. I walk in the eternal victory of the Cross. From this day forward, I will never look back. Backward—never. Forward—forever.

Degree and Declare: I am a citizen of Heaven. I live for Your Kingdom. **I walk in Your authority and power**. I receive the **full inheritance of health, peace, righteousness, Wealth, and provision, even eternal life.**

In Jesus' mighty name, I pray.

Amen.

BOOKS BY THIS AUTHOR

Deliverance By Fire: Unlocking The Courts, Thrones, And Altars Of True Freedom

A 7-Dimensional Manual for Self-Deliverance and Exorcism Ministry
By Anthony Mwangi — The BRANCH Seated in Zion

This prophetic manual is not just a teaching — it is a spiritual courtroom, an altar of judgment, and a throne of fire. Deliverance by Fire unveils the divine order of freedom as legislated in heaven's courts and manifested through the Spirit of Truth on earth.

Within these pages, you will encounter the architecture of true deliverance:
the Courts of Heaven, where accusations are silenced;
the Thrones of Dominion, where believers reign in Christ;
and the Altars of Fire, where covenants are purified and destinies reborn.

Built upon the revelation of the Seven Spirits of God, this book exposes the counterfeit thrones of darkness — and trains the sons and daughters of Zion to war by decree, not emotion; by the Word, not the flesh. Each chapter blends courtroom insight, prophetic instruction, and altar-based declarations to forge warriors of holiness and rest.

Through this 7-dimensional model — Spiritology, Soulogy,

Physiology, Theology, Chronology, Typology, and Technology — Anthony Mwangi reveals how the Spirit of Judgment and Burning restores divine order, purges bloodlines, and reclaims the altars of families, cities, and nations.

This book will teach you to:

Minister deliverance through heavenly legal protocol.

Break bloodline covenants and generational curses with the fire of truth.

Build Sabbath altars that sustain freedom and spiritual authority.

Operate in the courts of Zion, where Christ is both Judge and Advocate.

Move from manifestation to dominion — from reaction to legislation.

Deliverance by Fire is more than deliverance — it is reformation.

It is the blueprint of how heaven reclaims the earth through purified vessels who have become living stones and burning altars of the Spirit.

When you finish reading, you will not just understand deliverance — you will embody it.

The Armour Of Light: Unlocking The Mystery Of Divine Warfare

In the last days, the battlefield is no longer fought with swords and spears, but with light, truth, and the Spirit. The Armour of

Light: Unlocking the Mystery of Divine Warfare is a prophetic unveiling of God's end-time strategy for His chosen remnant.

This masterpiece reveals the hidden dimensions of the Word of God and the power of the Holy Spirit as the true armour that clothes, protects, and empowers the believer. Through spiritology, soulogy, physiology, and theology, the mystery of warfare is unfolded—showing how the Sabbath is God's dwelling place, the Courtroom of Heaven is His battlefield, and the Bride is His warrior.

Drawing from ancient truths and prophetic revelations, Anthony Mwangi — the BRANCH seated in Zion — uncovers the role of man in God's eternal judgment, the secret of Christ's blood as the light of warfare, and the revelation of the 7-dimensional Word as the weapon that disarms the dragon, the beast, and the false prophet.

This book is not just a teaching, but a weapon in itself. It equips the end-time believer to stand clothed in fire, sealed by the Spirit, and ready to triumph in the last battle.

If you are called to be part of the remnant, this is your manual of divine warfare.

Authority Over The Seven Demonic Nations: A Spiritual Eviction Manual For Gatekeepers

Authority Over the Seven Demonic Nations: A Spiritual Eviction Manual for Gatekeepers is a prophetic warfare guide designed to expose and overthrow the ancient strongholds that still occupy the gates of your life, family, and inheritance.

Based on Joshua 3:10, this book reveals the spiritual identities behind the seven Canaanite nations—territorial powers that

God commanded to be driven out. These are not just historical enemies; they are legal systems of defilement, fear, deception, generational bondage, pride, rejection, and dream manipulation.

Each nation is prophetically aligned with a ruling throne from the kingdom of darkness:

Canaanites – Lust / Defilement (Asmodeus)

Hittites – Wrath / Fear (Satan)

Hivites – Envy / Deception (Leviathan)

Perizzites – Sloth / Instability (Belphegor)

Girgashites – Greed / Ancestral Curses (Mammon)

Amorites – Pride / Domination (Lucifer)

Jebusites – Shame / Mockery (Beelzebub)

Through deep biblical revelation, courtroom language, and prophetic teaching, this manual will help you:

Identify the strongmen ruling over key gates in your life

Break legal rights and generational covenants that empower them

Rebuild spiritual altars and secure your inheritance

Activate your calling as a Gatekeeper in these last days

Pray elite-level courtroom decrees to dismantle demonic thrones

Whether you're a deliverance minister, prophetic intercessor, or believer hungry for spiritual authority, this book equips you to evict the enemy legally, spiritually, and permanently.

The thrones must fall. Your gates must be restored. Your territory must be cleansed.

ABOUT THE AUTHOR

Anthony Mwangi

Anthony Mwangi — The Branch Seated in Zion is a prophetic teacher, author, and visionary whose writings flow from the ancient rivers of wisdom, uniting Spirit, Scripture, and destiny. Rooted in the revelation of the 7 Dimensions of the Word of God, his ministry unveils the divine architecture of creation where light becomes law, and law becomes life.

As a scribe of fire, he carries a burden to restore Sabbath Order, tribal identity, and the government of the Spirit in this generation. His teachings draw from deep wells of Hebrew mystery, African prophetic lineage, and the eternal covenant of light written before the foundations of the world.

Through his works—including The Sabbath Is the Spirit, Stones of Fire, The River of Counsel, and The Scroll of Irathiro—Anthony calls forth a remnant priesthood: men and women refined as gold, awakened as stars, and established in Zion's holy mountain. The constellation of Christ — stars burning with love, rising with the Spirit's glory, filling the heavens of the earth with light. His words are not mere ink, but living fire breathed from the mountain, rekindling the ancient song of nations returning to their Creator, and declaring that Kenya, the land named after a mountain, stands as a sign of the Bright Morning Star returning.

He lives as a watchman of the dawn, carrying the scroll of Irathiro — testifying that the Word has returned to the East to finish the beginning.

PROPHETIC EPILOGUE: THE SCROLL OF IRATHIRO

The Scroll Unsealed — East to West, Genesis to Revelation

From the first light in Eden to the last light of Zion, the story of Irathiro is one continuous scroll. **Genesis 2** declared a garden planted *eastward*; **Revelation 22** unveils a river of life flowing from the throne. What began in the rising light of Eden is consummated in the eternal light of the Lamb.

The scroll was hidden through the ages, sealed from Adam to Abraham, from Israel to Christ. Yet in these last days, the seals are broken, and the mystery of the East is revealed. What was whispered in rivers, mountains, and stars is now proclaimed as the decree of the Lamb: *the stars of Irathiro shall reign forever in Zion.*

Kikuyu Prophecy Bound to Biblical Prophecy

The Kikuyu fathers looked eastward and called it **Irathiro**, the rising place of light. They built altars under fig and olive, awaiting the dawn. Without Torah or temple, they carried a seed of testimony, that the East is the womb of nations, the gateway of God's rising.

The prophets of Scripture spoke the same mystery:

- Eden planted eastward (**Genesis 2:8**).
- Abraham journeying eastward to the land of promise (**Genesis 12**).
- Ezekiel beholding glory from the east (**Ezekiel 43:2**).
- Christ born under a star rising in the east (**Matthew 2:2**).

Now the two streams meet; the African witness of Irathiro and the biblical testimony of the East converge into one scroll. The altar of Mount Kenya faces the same dawn as Mount Zion. The rivers of Tana and Ewaso Nyiro echo the streams of **Psalm 46:4**. The prophecy of the Kikuyu is sealed together with the prophecy of Israel, and both rise in the Lamb.

The Final Decree — Stars from Irathiro Reign in Zion

The scroll closes with fire, yet not with silence. A decree resounds from Zion's throne:

> *"The Stars from Irathiro shall reign forever in Zion.*
> *The eastward rising is fulfilled in the Bright Morning Star.*
> *The Bride is crowned, the dragon cast down, the beast judged, Babylon fallen, and the Lamb exalted.*
> *Africa's womb has given forth light, and Zion's constellation shines unending.*
> *There is no more night, for the Lord God gives them light:*

and they shall reign for ever and ever." (cf. Revelation 22:5)

The Scroll of Irathiro is sealed in fire.
It is the witness of Eden, the covenant of Abraham, the crown of Israel, the rising of Christ, the outpouring of Pentecost, the mandate of Africa, and the throne of Zion.
From Genesis to Revelation, from Kenya to Jerusalem, the decree stands: **the stars of Irathiro shall shine forever in the Lamb's eternal day.**

AFTERWORD

The Scroll Has Been Unsealed

The journey of this scroll is not an ending, it is a summoning. Every word within these pages was written to awaken remembrance, to ignite the lamp that once burned before the throne. The light of Irathiro does not fade; it multiplies through those who read, believe, and arise.

From the mountains of whiteness to the rivers of counsel, the Spirit of the Lord still moves upon the face of the deep, calling His sons and daughters back to the covenant of origin. This is not the work of man, but of the eternal Breath who speaks through dust and fire, shaping nations once again.

Gold, frankincense, and myrrh still travel in the hands of those who carry revelation, intercession, and sacrifice. The East still shines. The King still reigns. And the Word still writes itself in living hearts.

So let the reader become the voice. Let the student become the flame. Let the nations behold the light of Irathiro rising again. For the time is come: **the scroll is open, and Zion remembers her song.**

ACKNOWLEDGEMENT

First, I lift my gratitude to the **Ancient of Days**, the Father of Lights, from whom every good and perfect gift descends. Without His breath, no star can rise.

To **Jesus Christ, the Bright and Morning Star**, who gave me both the vision and the courage to write — this book is His testimony shining through these pages.

To the **Holy Spirit**, my Teacher and Comforter, who revealed the mysteries of Irathiro, guiding me through the Scriptures precept upon precept, line upon line, until the hidden things of old came alive.

I acknowledge the **cloud of witnesses** who went before us — Abraham who counted the stars, Jacob who saw the ladder, Joseph who dreamed of the sun, moon, and stars, Daniel who saw the wise shining, and John who beheld the Bride crowned with stars. Their lives still speak.

I honor my **family and spiritual covering**, whose prayers, patience, and encouragement became the oil for this fire.

I bless my **nation, Kenya**, and the peoples of Africa, for carrying within their tongue and prophecy the mystery of *Irathiro*. This is a sign of God's purpose in these last days.

And finally, to every reader who has taken this journey: I acknowledge you. You are not reading by chance. You are a rising star in God's constellation, called to shine in the East Gate of

Zion.

May the LORD Himself engrave these words in your spirit.

THE RISING OF IRATHIRO

In the beginning, God planted His garden eastward in Eden — a whisper of origin, a direction of light. From that first sunrise, every covenant, every promise, every star was drawn eastward, toward awakening. Irathiro "the rising" is not a place alone; it is a prophecy, a heartbeat that began in Eden and now echoes in Africa.

The story of the stars is the story of man's return to light. From Abraham's gaze upon the heavens, counting stars as heirs, to the vision of John beholding a Woman crowned with twelve, the testimony remains: God writes His promise in the firmament. Each constellation speaks of covenant; each dawn reminds the world that glory still rises in the East.

This book is born from that dawn. It gathers the hidden seed of Genesis, the fire of Pentecost, and the shining of Zion into one unbroken revelation that the Spirit has chosen a people, a mountain, a moment. Kenya, the mountain nation of whiteness, stands as a final witness of Irathiro: the east star of the earth, where prayer becomes light and the nations behold the glory of the Lamb.

The rising is not new; it is ancient light remembered. It is the Sabbath of nations, the rest of the Spirit returning to its throne. And as the Bright Morning Star ascends, His reflection multiplies sons and daughters shining as constellations of fire.

Irathiro has risen. The East has spoken. The stars are home again.

www.ingramcontent.com/pod-product-compliance
Lightning Source LLC
Chambersburg PA
CBHW070155100426
42743CB00013B/2918